Developing Nations and the Politics of Global Integration

Integrating National Economies: Promise and Pitfalls

Barry Bosworth (Brookings Institution) and Gur Ofer (Hebrew University)
Reforming Planned Economies in an Integrating World Economy

Ralph C. Bryant (Brookings Institution)
International Coordination of National Stabilization Policies

Susan M. Collins (Brookings Institution/Georgetown University)
Distributive Issues: A Constraint on Global Integration

Richard N. Cooper (Harvard University)
Environment and Resource Policies for the World Economy

Ronald G. Ehrenberg (Cornell University)
Labor Markets and Integrating National Economies

Barry Eichengreen (University of California, Berkeley)
International Monetary Arrangements for the 21st Century

Mitsuhiro Fukao (Bank of Japan)
Financial Integration, Corporate Governance, and the Performance of Multinational Companies

Stephan Haggard (University of California, San Diego)
Developing Nations and the Politics of Global Integration

Richard J. Herring (University of Pennsylvania) and Robert E. Litan (Department of Justice/Brookings Institution)
Financial Regulation in the Global Economy

Miles Kahler (University of California, San Diego)
International Institutions and the Political Economy of Integration

Anne O. Krueger (Stanford University)
Trade Policies and Developing Nations

Robert Z. Lawrence (Harvard University)
Regionalism, Multilateralism, and Deeper Integration

Sylvia Ostry (University of Toronto) and Richard R. Nelson (Columbia University)
Techno-Nationalism and Techno-Globalism: Conflict and Cooperation

Robert L. Paarlberg (Wellesley College/Harvard University)
Leadership Abroad Begins at Home: U.S. Foreign Economic Policy after the Cold War

Peter Rutland (Wesleyan University)
Russia, Eurasia, and the Global Economy

F. M. Scherer (Harvard University)
Competition Policies for an Integrated World Economy

Susan L. Shirk (University of California, San Diego)
How China Opened Its Door: The Political Success of the PRC's Foreign Trade and Investment Reforms

Alan O. Sykes (University of Chicago)
Product Standards for Internationally Integrated Goods Markets

Akihiko Tanaka (Institute of Oriental Culture, University of Tokyo)
The Politics of Deeper Integration: National Attitudes and Policies in Japan

Vito Tanzi (International Monetary Fund)
Taxation in an Integrating World

William Wallace (St. Antony's College, Oxford University)
Regional Integration: The West European Experience

Stephan Haggard

Developing Nations and the Politics of Global Integration

THE BROOKINGS INSTITUTION
Washington, D.C.

Library of Congress Cataloging-in-Publication data:
Haggard, Stephan
Developing nations and the politics of global integration/
Stephan Haggard
p. cm.—(Integrating national economies)
Includes bibliographical references and index.
ISBN 0-8157-3390-9 (cl).—ISBN 0-8157-3389-5 (pa.)
1. Developing countries—Economic integration. 2. Developing
countries—Economic conditions. 3. Developing countries—Economic
policy. 4. Developing countries—Foreign economic relations.
5. International economic relations. I. Title. II. Series.
HC59.7.H274 1995
337.1′1724—dc20   94-44251
                                                        CIP

9 8 7 6 5 4 3 2 1

The paper used in this publication meets the minimum requirements of
American National Standard for Information Sciences—Permanence of Paper
for Printed Library Materials, ANSI Z39.48-1984

Typeset in Plantin

Composition by Princeton Editorial Associates
Princeton, New Jersey

Printed by R. R. Donnelley and Sons Co.
Harrisonburg, Virginia

Foreword

MANY developing countries have recently joined the more economically advanced nations in liberalizing trade and in taking steps to deepen global integration. Are the reforms by the developing countries politically consolidated, or will political upheaval derail them?

In this book, Stephan Haggard examines the position of the developing countries in the international trade regime, focusing on the middle-income nations of East and Southeast Asia and Latin America. Various international constraints—economic shocks as well as multilateral and bilateral political pressures—have pushed these countries toward economic liberalization and into economic relations with advanced industrial states. Although the domestic political consensus for these changes is relatively firm in East and Southeast Asia, it is tenuous in Latin America and India, where policy reforms have been sudden and difficult.

One current controversy centers on whether the developing countries will join closed regional blocs that will fragment the international economy. Haggard argues that the advanced developing countries have become strong supporters of the multilateral system and that the extent of discriminatory regionalism has been overstated. A more serious threat is the lure of bilateralism and the effort of the advanced industrial states to impose standards on developing countries that are inappropriate or politically counterproductive.

Stephan Haggard is professor at the Graduate School of International Relations and Pacific Studies at the University of California, San Diego. He received helpful advice or comments on the manuscript from Jagdish Bhagwati, Ralph Bryant, Susan Collins, Sebastian Edwards, Miles Kahler, Robert R. Kaufman, Anne Krueger, Robert Lawrence, Sylvia Maxfield, and Carol Wise, and from participants at the Brookings meeting at which sections of the book were first presented. He is also indebted to Barbara Stallings for ideas developed in the context of a joint research project on the politics of adjustment. He wishes to thank a hardworking team of research assistants: Ed Chan, Michelle Chang, Matthew Harrel, Steve McCarthy, Joseph Perez, Martin Stein, and Craig Tobey.

At Brookings, Theresa Walker edited the manuscript and Laura Kelly verified it. Kathey Bucholz, Lisa Guillory, Sara Hufham, and Paige Offinger assisted in typing the manuscript. Princeton Editorial Associates prepared the index.

Funding for the project came from the Center for Global Partnership of the Japan Foundation, the Curry Foundation, the Ford Foundation, the Korea Foundation, the Tokyo Club Foundation for Global Studies, the United States–Japan Foundation, and the Alex C. Walker Educational and Charitable Foundation. The author and Brookings are grateful for their support.

The views expressed in this book are those of the authors and should not be ascribed to any of the persons or organizations acknowledged above, or to the trustees, officers, or staff members of the Brookings Institution.

BRUCE K. MACLAURY
President

February 1995
Washington, D.C.

Contents

Preface to the Studies on Integrating National Economies

*E*CONOMIC interdependence among nations has increased sharply in the past half century. For example, while the value of total production of industrial countries increased at a rate of about 9 percent a year on average between 1964 and 1992, the value of the exports of those nations grew at an average rate of 12 percent, and lending and borrowing across national borders through banks surged upward even more rapidly at 23 percent a year. This international economic interdependence has contributed to significantly improved standards of living for most countries. Continuing international economic integration holds out the promise of further benefits. Yet the increasing sensitivity of national economies to events and policies originating abroad creates dilemmas and pitfalls if national policies and international cooperation are poorly managed.

The Brookings Project on Integrating National Economies, of which this study is a component, focuses on the interplay between two fundamental facts about the world at the end of the twentieth century. First, the world will continue for the foreseeable future to be organized politically into nation-states with sovereign governments. Second, increasing economic integration among nations will continue to erode differences among national economies and undermine the autonomy of national governments. The project explores the opportunities and tensions arising from these two facts.

Scholars from a variety of disciplines have produced twenty-one studies for the first phase of the project. Each study examines the heightened competition between national political sovereignty and increased cross-border economic integration. This preface identifies background themes and issues common to all the studies and provides a brief overview of the project as a whole.[1]

Increasing World Economic Integration

Two underlying sets of causes have led nations to become more closely intertwined. First, technological, social, and cultural changes have sharply reduced the effective economic distances among nations. Second, many of the government policies that traditionally inhibited cross-border transactions have been relaxed or even dismantled.

The same improvements in transportation and communications technology that make it much easier and cheaper for companies in New York to ship goods to California, for residents of Strasbourg to visit relatives in Marseilles, and for investors in Hokkaido to buy and sell shares on the Tokyo Stock Exchange facilitate trade, migration, and capital movements spanning nations and continents. The sharply reduced costs of moving goods, money, people, and information underlie the profound economic truth that technology has made the world markedly smaller.

New communications technology has been especially significant for financial activity. Computers, switching devices, and telecommunications satellites have slashed the cost of transmitting information internationally, of confirming transactions, and of paying for transactions. In the 1950s, for example, foreign exchange could be bought and sold only during conventional business hours in the initiating party's time zone. Such transactions can now be carried out instantaneously twenty-four hours a day. Large banks pass the management of their worldwide foreign-exchange positions around the globe from one branch to another, staying continuously ahead of the setting sun.

Such technological innovations have increased the knowledge of potentially profitable international exchanges and of economic opportunities abroad. Those developments, in turn, have changed consumers' and producers' tastes. Foreign goods, foreign vacations, foreign financial investments—virtually anything from other nations—have lost some of their exotic character.

---

1. A complete list of authors and study titles is included at the beginning of this volume, facing the title page.

Although technological change permits increased contact among nations, it would not have produced such dramatic effects if it had been countermanded by government policies. Governments have traditionally taxed goods moving in international trade, directly restricted imports and subsidized exports, and tried to limit international capital movements. Those policies erected "separation fences" at the borders of nations. From the perspective of private sector agents, separation fences imposed extra costs on cross-border transactions. They reduced trade and, in some cases, eliminated it. During the 1930s governments used such policies with particular zeal, a practice now believed to have deepened and lengthened the Great Depression.

After World War II, most national governments began—sometimes unilaterally, more often collaboratively—to lower their separation fences, to make them more permeable, or sometimes even to tear down parts of them. The multilateral negotiations under the auspices of the General Agreement on Trade and Tariffs (GATT)—for example, the Kennedy Round in the 1960s, the Tokyo Round in the 1970s, and most recently the protracted negotiations of the Uruguay Round, formally signed only in April 1994—stand out as the most prominent examples of fence lowering for trade in goods. Though contentious and marked by many compromises, the GATT negotiations are responsible for sharp reductions in at-the-border restrictions on trade in goods and services. After the mid-1980s a large number of developing countries moved unilaterally to reduce border barriers and to pursue outwardly oriented policies.

The lowering of fences for financial transactions began later and was less dramatic. Nonetheless, by the 1990s government restrictions on capital flows, especially among the industrial countries, were much less important and widespread than at the end of World War II and in the 1950s.

By shrinking the economic distances among nations, changes in technology would have progressively integrated the world economy even in the absence of reductions in governments' separation fences. Reductions in separation fences would have enhanced interdependence even without the technological innovations. Together, these two sets of evolutionary changes have reinforced each other and strikingly transformed the world economy.

Changes in the Government of Nations

Simultaneously with the transformation of the global economy, major changes have occurred in the world's political structure. First, the number of governmental decisionmaking units in the world has expanded markedly, and political power has been diffused more broadly among them. Rising nationalism and, in some areas, heightened ethnic tensions have accompanied that increasing political pluralism.

The history of membership in international organizations documents the sharp growth in the number of independent states. For example, only 44 nations participated in the Bretton Woods conference of July 1944, which gave birth to the International Monetary Fund. But by the end of 1970, the IMF had 118 member nations. The number of members grew to 150 by the mid-1980s and to 178 by December 1993. Much of this growth reflects the collapse of colonial empires. Although many nations today are small and carry little individual weight in the global economy, their combined influence is considerable, and their interests cannot be ignored as easily as they were in the past.

A second political trend, less visible but equally important, has been the gradual loss of the political and economic hegemony of the United States. Immediately after World War II, the United States by itself accounted for more than one-third of world production. By the early 1990s the U.S. share had fallen to about one-fifth. Concurrently, the political and economic influence of the European colonial powers continued to wane, and the economic significance of nations outside Europe and North America, such as Japan, Korea, Indonesia, China, Brazil, and Mexico, increased. A world in which economic power and influence are widely diffused has displaced a world in which one or a few nations effectively dominated international decisionmaking.

Turmoil and the prospect of fundamental change in the formerly centrally planned economies compose a third factor causing radical changes in world politics. During the era of central planning, governments in those nations tried to limit external influences on their economies. Now leaders in the formerly planned economies are trying to adopt reforms modeled on Western capitalist principles. To the extent that these efforts succeed, those nations will increase their economic involvement with the rest of the world. Political and economic alignments among the Western industrialized nations will be forced to adapt.

Governments and scholars have begun to assess these three trends, but their far-reaching ramifications will not be clear for decades.

Dilemmas for National Policies

Cross-border economic integration and national political sovereignty have increasingly come into conflict, leading to a growing mismatch between the economic and political structures of the world. The effective domains of economic markets have come to coincide less and less with national governmental jurisdictions.

When the separation fences at nations' borders were high, governments and citizens could sharply distinguish "international" from "domestic" policies. International policies dealt with at-the-border barriers, such as tariffs and quotas, or responded to events occurring abroad. In contrast, domestic policies were concerned with everything behind the nation's borders, such as competition and antitrust rules, corporate governance, product standards, worker safety, regulation and supervision of financial institutions, environmental protection, tax codes, and the government's budget. Domestic policies were regarded as matters about which nations were sovereign, to be determined by the preferences of the nation's citizens and its political institutions, without regard for effects on other nations.

As separation fences have been lowered and technological innovations have shrunk economic distances, a multitude of formerly neglected differences among nations' domestic policies have become exposed to international scrutiny. National governments and international negotiations must thus increasingly deal with "deeper"—behind-the-border—integration. For example, if country A permits companies to emit air and water pollutants whereas country B does not, companies that use pollution-generating methods of production will find it cheaper to produce in country A. Companies in country B that compete internationally with companies in country A are likely to complain that foreign competitors enjoy unfair advantages and to press for international pollution standards.

Deeper integration requires analysis of the economic and the political aspects of virtually all nonborder policies and practices. Such issues have already figured prominently in negotiations over the evolution of the European Community, over the Uruguay Round of GATT negotiations, over the North American Free Trade Agreement (NAFTA), and over the bilateral economic relationships between Japan and the United States. Future debates about behind-the-border policies will occur with increasing frequency and prove at least as complex and contentious as the past negotiations regarding at-the-border restrictions.

Tensions about deeper integration arise from three broad sources: cross-border spillovers, diminished national autonomy, and challenges to political sovereignty.

Cross-Border Spillovers

Some activities in one nation produce consequences that spill across borders and affect other nations. Illustrations of these spillovers abound. Given the impact of modern technology of banking and securities markets in creating interconnected networks, lax rules in one nation erode the ability of all other nations to enforce banking and securities rules and to deal with fraudulent transactions. Given the rapid diffusion of knowledge, science and technology policies in one nation generate knowledge that other nations can use without full payment. Labor market policies become matters of concern to other nations because workers migrate in search of work; policies in one nation can trigger migration that floods or starves labor markets elsewhere. When one nation dumps pollutants into the air or water that other nations breathe or drink, the matter goes beyond the unitary concern of the polluting nation and becomes a matter for international negotiation. Indeed, the hydrocarbons that are emitted into the atmosphere when individual nations burn coal for generating electricity contribute to global warming and are thereby a matter of concern for the entire world.

The tensions associated with cross-border spillovers can be especially vexing when national policies generate outcomes alleged to be competitively inequitable, as in the example in which country A permits companies to emit pollutants and country B does not. Or consider a situation in which country C requires commodities, whether produced at home or abroad, to meet certain design standards, justified for safety reasons. Foreign competitors may find it too expensive to meet these standards. In that event, the standards in C act very much like tariffs or quotas, effectively narrowing or even eliminating foreign competition for domestic producers. Citing examples of this sort, producers or governments in individual nations often complain that business is not conducted on a "level playing field." Typically, the complaining nation proposes that *other* nations adjust their policies to moderate or remove the competitive inequities.

Arguments for creating a level playing field are troublesome at best. International trade occurs precisely because of differences among nations—in resource endowments, labor skills, and consumer tastes. Nations specialize in producing goods and services in which they are relatively most efficient. In a fundamental sense, cross-border trade is valuable because the playing field is *not* level.

When David Ricardo first developed the theory of comparative advantage, he focused on differences among nations owing to climate or technology. But Ricardo could as easily have ascribed the productive differences to differing "social climates" as to physical or technological climates. Taking all "climatic" differences as given, the theory of comparative advantage argues that free trade among nations will maximize global welfare.

Taken to its logical extreme, the notion of leveling the playing field implies that nations should become homogeneous in all major respects. But that recommendation is unrealistic and even pernicious. Suppose country A decides that it is too poor to afford the costs of a clean environment, and will thus permit the production of goods that pollute local air and water supplies. Or suppose it concludes that it cannot afford stringent protections for worker safety. Country A will then argue that it is inappropriate for other nations to impute to country A the value they themselves place on a clean environment and safety standards (just as it would be inappropriate to impute the A valuations to the environment of other nations). The core of the idea of political sovereignty is to permit national residents to order their lives and property in accord with their own preferences.

Which perspective about differences among nations in behind-the-border policies is more compelling? Is country A merely exercising its national preferences and appropriately exploiting its comparative advantage in goods that are dirty or dangerous to produce? Or does a legitimate international problem exist that justifies pressure from other nations urging country A to accept changes in its policies (thus curbing its national sovereignty)? When national governments negotiate resolutions to such questions—trying to agree whether individual nations are legitimately exercising sovereign choices or, alternatively, engaging in behavior that is unfair or damaging to other nations—the dialogue is invariably contentious because the resolutions depend on the typically complex circumstances of the international spillovers and on the relative weights accorded to the interests of particular individuals and particular nations.

Diminished National Autonomy

As cross-border economic integration increases, governments experience greater difficulties in trying to control events within their borders. Those difficulties, summarized by the term *diminished autonomy*, are the second set of reasons why tensions arise from the competition between political sovereignty and economic integration.

For example, nations adjust monetary and fiscal policies to influence domestic inflation and employment. In setting these policies, smaller countries have always been somewhat constrained by foreign economic events and policies. Today, however, all nations are constrained, often severely. More than in the past, therefore, nations may be better able to achieve their economic goals if they work together collaboratively in adjusting their macroeconomic policies.

Diminished autonomy and cross-border spillovers can sometimes be allowed to persist without explicit international cooperation to deal with them. States in the United States adopt their own tax systems and set policies for assistance to poor single people without any formal cooperation or limitation. Market pressures operate to force a degree of de facto cooperation. If one state taxes corporations too heavily, it knows business will move elsewhere. (Those familiar with older debates about "fiscal federalism" within the United States and other nations will recognize the similarity between those issues and the emerging international debates about deeper integration of national economies.) Analogously, differences among nations in regulations, standards, policies, institutions, and even social and cultural preferences create economic incentives for a kind of arbitrage that erodes or eliminates the differences. Such pressures involve not only the conventional arbitrage that exploits price differentials (buying at one point in geographic space or time and selling at another) but also shifts in the location of production facilities and in the residence of factors of production.

In many other cases, however, cross-border spillovers, arbitrage pressures, and diminished effectiveness of national policies can produce unwanted consequences. In cases involving what economists call externalities (external economies and diseconomies), national governments may need to cooperate to promote mutual interests. For example, population growth, continued urbanization, and the more intensive exploitation of natural resources generate external diseconomies not only within but across national boundaries. External economies generated when benefits spill across national jurisdictions probably also increase in importance (for instance, the gains from basic research and from control of communicable diseases).

None of these situations is new, but technological change and the reduction of tariffs and quotas heighten their importance. When one nation produces goods (such as scientific research) or "bads" (such as pollution) that significantly affect other nations, individual governments acting sequentially and noncooperatively cannot deal effectively with the resulting issues. In the absence of explicit cooperation and political leadership, too few collective goods and too many collective bads will be supplied.

Challenges to Political Sovereignty

The pressures from cross-border economic integration sometimes even lead individuals or governments to challenge the core assumptions of national political sovereignty. Such challenges are a third source of tensions about deeper integration.

The existing world system of nation-states assumes that a nation's residents are free to follow their own values and to select their own political arrangements without interference from others. Similarly, property rights are allocated by nation. (The so-called global commons, such as outer space and the deep seabed, are the sole exceptions.) A nation is assumed to have the sovereign right to exploit its property in accordance with its own preferences and policies. Political sovereignty is thus analogous to the concept of consumer sovereignty (the presumption that the individual consumer best knows his or her own interests and should exercise them freely).

In times of war, some nations have had sovereignty wrested from them by force. In earlier eras, a handful of individuals or groups have questioned the premises of political sovereignty. With the profound increases in economic integration in recent decades, however, a larger number of individuals and groups—and occasionally even their national governments—have identified circumstances in which, it is claimed, some universal or international set of values should take precedence over the preferences or policies of particular nations.

Some groups seize on human-rights issues, for example, or what they deem to be egregiously inappropriate political arrangements in other nations. An especially prominent case occurred when citizens in many nations labeled the former apartheid policies of South Africa an affront to universal values and emphasized that the South African government was not legitimately representing the interests of a majority of South Africa's residents. Such views caused many national governments to apply economic sanctions against South Africa. Examples of value conflicts are not restricted to human rights, however. Groups focusing on environmental issues characterize tropical rain forests as the lungs of the world and the genetic repository for numerous species of plants and animals that are the heritage of all mankind. Such views lead Europeans, North Americans, or Japanese to challenge the timber-cutting policies of Brazilians and Indonesians. A recent controversy over tuna fishing with long drift nets that kill porpoises is yet another example. Environmentalists in the United States whose sensibilities were offended by the drowning of porpoises required U.S. boats at some additional expense to amend their fishing practices. The U.S. fishermen, complaining about imported tuna caught with less regard for porpoises, persuaded the U.S. government to ban such tuna imports (both direct imports from the countries in which the tuna is caught and indirect imports shipped via third countries). Mexico and Venezuela were the main countries affected by this ban; a GATT dispute panel sided with Mexico against the United States in the controversy, which further upset the U.S. environmental community.

A common feature of all such examples is the existence, real or alleged, of "psychological externalities" or "political failures." Those holding such views reject untrammeled political sovereignty for nation-states in deference to universal or non-national values. They wish to constrain the exercise of individual nations' sovereignties through international negotiations or, if necessary, by even stronger intervention.

The Management of International Convergence

In areas in which arbitrage pressures and cross-border spillovers are weak and psychological or political externalities are largely absent, national governments may encounter few problems with deeper integration. Diversity across nations may persist quite easily. But at the other extreme, arbitrage and spillovers in some areas may be so strong that they threaten to erode national diversity completely. Or psychological and political sensitivities may be asserted too powerfully to be ignored. Governments will then be confronted with serious tensions, and national policies and behaviors may eventually converge to common, worldwide patterns (for example, subject to internationally agreed norms or minimum standards). Eventual convergence across nations, if it occurs, could happen in a harmful way (national policies and practices being driven to a least common denominator with externalities ignored, in effect a "race to the bottom") or it could occur with mutually beneficial results ("survival of the fittest and the best").

Each study in this series addresses basic questions about the management of international convergence: if, when, and how national governments should intervene to try to influence the consequences of arbitrage pressures, cross-border spillovers, diminished autonomy, and the assertion of psychological or political externalities. A wide variety of responses is conceivable. We identify six, which should be regarded not as distinct categories but as ranges along a continuum.

National autonomy defines a situation at one end of the continuum in which national governments make decentralized decisions with little or no consultation and no explicit cooperation. This response represents political sovereignty at its strongest, undiluted by any international management of convergence.

Mutual recognition, like national autonomy, presumes decentralized decisions by national governments and relies on market competition to guide the process of international convergence. Mutual recognition, however, entails exchanges of information and consultations among governments to constrain the formation of national regulations and policies. As understood in discussions of economic integration within the European Community, moreover, mutual recognition entails an explicit acceptance by each member nation of the regulations, standards, and certification procedures of other members. For example, mutual recognition allows wine or liquor produced in any European Union country to be sold in all twelve member countries even if production standards in member countries differ. Doctors licensed in France are permitted to practice in Germany, and vice versa, even if licensing procedures in the two countries differ.

Governments may agree on rules that restrict their freedom to set policy or that promote gradual convergence in the structure of policy. As international consultations and monitoring of compliance with such rules become more important, this situation can be described as *monitored decentralization*. The Group of Seven finance ministers meetings, supplemented by the IMF's surveillance over exchange rate and macroeconomic policies, illustrate this approach to management.

Coordination goes further than mutual recognition and monitored decentralization in acknowledging convergence pressures. It is also more ambitious in promoting intergovernmental cooperation to deal with them. Coordination involves jointly designed mutual adjustments of national policies. In clear-cut cases of coordination, bargaining occurs and governments agree to behave differently from the ways they would have behaved without the agreement. Examples include the World Health Organization's procedures for controlling communicable diseases and the 1987 Montreal Protocol (to a 1985 framework convention) for the protection of stratospheric ozone by reducing emissions of chlorofluorocarbons.

Explicit harmonization, which requires still higher levels of intergovernmental cooperation, may require agreement on regional standards or world standards. Explicit harmonization typically entails still greater departures from decentralization in decisionmaking and still further strengthening of international institutions. The 1988 agreement among major central banks to set minimum standards for the required capital positions of commercial banks (reached through the Committee on Banking Regulations and Supervisory Practices at the Bank for International Settlements) is an example of partially harmonized regulations.

At the opposite end of the spectrum from national autonomy lies *federalist mutual governance*, which implies continuous bargaining and joint, centralized decisionmaking. To make federalist mutual governance work would require greatly strengthened supranational institutions. This end of the management spectrum, now relevant only as an analytical benchmark, is a possible outcome that can be imagined for the middle or late decades of the twenty-first century, possibly even sooner for regional groupings like the European Union.

Overview of the Brookings Project

Despite their growing importance, the issues of deeper economic integration and its competition with national political sovereignty were largely neglected in the 1980s. In 1992 the Brookings Institution initiated its project on Integrating National Economies to direct attention to these important questions.

In studying this topic, Brookings sought and received the co-operation of some of the world's leading economists, political scientists, foreign-policy specialists, and government officials, representing all regions of the world. Although some functional areas require a special focus on European, Japanese, and North American perspectives, at all junctures the goal was to include, in addition, the perspectives of developing nations and the formerly centrally planned economies.

The first phase of the project commissioned the twenty-one scholarly studies listed at the beginning of the book. One or two lead discussants, typically residents of parts of the world other than the area where the author resides, were asked to comment on each study.

Authors enjoyed substantial freedom to design their individual studies, taking due account of the overall themes and goals of the project. The guidelines for the studies requested that at least some of the analysis be carried out with a non-normative perspective. In effect, authors were asked to develop a "baseline" of what might happen in the absence of changed policies or further international cooperation. For their normative analyses, authors were asked to start with an agnostic posture that did not prejudge the net benefits or costs resulting from integration. The project organizers themselves had no presumption about whether national diversity is better or worse than international convergence or about what the individual studies should conclude regarding the desirability of increased integration. On the contrary, each author was asked to address the trade-offs in his or her issue area between diversity and convergence and to locate the area, currently and prospectively, on the spectrum of international management possibilities running between national autonomy through mutual recognition to coordination and explicit harmonization.

HENRY J. AARON   SUSAN M. COLLINS
RALPH C. BRYANT   ROBERT Z. LAWRENCE

Chapter 1

Deep Integration and the Developing World

THE developing countries have historically viewed closer economic and political integration with the advanced industrial states with ambivalence if not outright skepticism. The developing countries have generally benefited from the lowering of barriers to world trade and the growth of foreign investment, but close ties to the world economy were also seen as creating vulnerabilities, including risks of dependence and political interference. The multilateral economic institutions—the General Agreement on Tariffs and Trade (GATT), the World Bank, and the International Monetary Fund (IMF)—were also the locus of substantial ambivalence. Strong international rules governing trade could in principle constrain the strong and protect the weak, and the multilateral provision of finance had obvious benefits. But the developing countries have also viewed the Bretton Woods institutions as exclusive clubs of the rich and as instruments for the imposition of unwarranted policy conditionality.

Long encompassing countries at very different levels of development and with widely divergent problems and interests, differences among the nations of the third world on these questions became more marked during the 1980s. Some countries, particularly in East and Southeast Asia, continued to grow rapidly by maintaining close ties to the world economy. The middle-income countries of Latin America experienced severe shocks and responded with wide-ranging economic reform efforts that reversed decades of inward-looking policies. Other poorer developing countries, especially in Africa, faced even more daunting problems than did Latin America during the "lost decade" of the 1980s and remained heavily dependent on international largesse.

1

These differences in level of development and economic circumstance affected the stance that countries took toward deeper economic integration. Some advanced developing countries are becoming important players in the trading system and as a result have come under strong pressure to conform with international norms. Poorer countries concentrated on achieving "shallow" integration through removing trade and investment barriers. Their prospects for deeper integration through international policy coordination are complicated by these efforts, or the agenda is simply more remote from the problems they face.

The International Politics of Deep Integration

Integration is frequently used as a synonym for interdependence to refer to the extent and depth of economic transactions among nations. In this book, integration refers to the fundamentally political process of policy coordination and adjustment designed to facilitate closer economic interdependence and to manage the externalities that arise from it.[1] Analysis of such cooperation has typically focused on "shallow integration": the relaxation of border restrictions on trade and investment and the granting of national treatment for products and firms. As shallow integration has proceeded, however, numerous "behind-the-border" policies—policies once deemed wholly domestic—have become the subject of international negotiations; the coordination of these policies constitutes deep integration.

The ambitious agenda for deeper integration among advanced industrial states ranges from harmonization of standards to macroeconomic policy coordination. The idea of deep integration is especially advanced in Europe, where the process extends well beyond coordination of national policies to the development of *regional* political institutions and policies.

Three components of the deep integration agenda have relevance for the developing countries. The first is the effort to extend international rules from trade to investment. Trade-related investment measures (TRIMs) were on the agenda of the new GATT round.[2] Much

---

1. This definition follows the work of political scientists, particularly Keohane (1984).
2. See Ostry (1990); Cowhey and Aronson (1993).

of the debate about "trade" in services is really about national treatment for foreign firms. Regional initiatives in Europe and North America center as much on the promotion and regulation of investment as they do on trade. The explosion of foreign direct investment in the second half of the 1980s and the close links between trade and investment have inevitably drawn national governments into efforts to guarantee market access and national treatment for their multinational enterprises.

The second related concern of the new agenda that is of particular relevance to developing countries is how and whether to address differences in national regulatory regimes that have discriminatory effects on trade and investment or that generate "unfair" competition. These concerns encompass rules governing intellectual property, differences in national standards, and financial, industrial, technology, competition, and environmental policies.

Recently, the debate on deep integration has expanded to include a third, and even more complex, set of conflicts that Sylvia Ostry and Richard Nelson have labeled system friction: how differences in national corporate, industrial, and even political structures constitute restraints on trade and investment.[3] The EC's 1983 call for a GATT working party on Japan and the discussion of the Japanese retail system and keiretsu form of business organization under the U.S.-Japan Structural Impediments Initiative exemplify this trend.[4]

For the purposes of this study, these three clusters of issues constitute the deep integration agenda.[5] The rules governing foreign direct investment are usually considered a component of shallow integration, since they involve the removal of at-the-border barriers and the extension of the principle of national treatment contained in article II of GATT from traded goods to the rights of foreign firms. For the developing countries, however, improving the climate for foreign investment is typically bound up with wider regulatory changes re-

3. See Ostry and Nelson (1995); Kahler (1993).

4. The EC complaint focused not only on visible and invisible trade and investment barriers but on how the concentration and interlinking of production, finance, and distribution structures created an imbalance in contracting parties' access to GATT benefits. See also Schoppa (1993); McMillan (1994).

5. Macroeconomic policy coordination has also been considered under the "deep integration" rubric but is less salient for the developing countries and is not considered here. It is considered by several other studies in this project, particularly Bryant (forthcoming).

quired to bring national practices into line with those in the advanced industrial states; for this reason, I consider the rules governing such investment a component of the deep integration agenda.

Deep integration implies precisely the adjustment of national policies around a negotiated norm. From a normative perspective, the question is whether deep integration constitutes a worthy goal. Should nations tolerate national regulatory differences, rely on the traditional arsenal of unfair trade laws to manage them, or move toward more ambitious forms of international cooperation? Such cooperation might range from the negotiation of minimal standards to the harmonization of national policies and could take place at the bilateral, regional, or multilateral level.

For political economists, however, analysis centers on explaining the extent of such cooperation and identifying the institutional form it takes. How does the agenda for deep integration get set in the first place? Why do countries seek or resist such international cooperation? At what level are agreements negotiated, and what determines the extent of compliance with them?

There are both economic and political reasons to think that, the deep integration agenda would be neither germane nor agreeable to developing countries. It is not clear that the negotiation of deeper integration is necessarily in the interests of the developing countries. Strong arguments are made about the positive welfare benefits to be gained from shallow integration, but there is very little theory about whether regulatory convergence represents an optimal policy for a country or for the world as a whole. In areas such as intellectual property, the environment, and labor standards developing countries could suffer if harmonization occurred around the norms of developed countries, particularly if convergence were enforced through sanctions.[6]

The political economy of the developing countries would not lead one to expect an open embrace of the deep integration agenda either. With few exceptions, the developing countries have pursued growth strategies characterized by persistent macroeconomic imbalances and extensive state intervention. As a result, many developing countries are still seeking to consolidate macroeconomic stabilization, balance of payments adjustment, and basic reforms of the trade and exchange

---

6. This point is made strongly by Krueger (forthcoming).

rate regime.[7] The pursuit of these reforms does not logically foreclose simultaneous moves toward deep integration. But given the large divergence in national policies between developed and developing countries, especially on regulatory issues, deep integration would imply a reform process that is more comprehensive and thus more demanding.

The discussion of new forms of international policy coordination among the advanced industrial states takes place in a context in which domestic interests have converged to a great extent around a relatively open posture toward the world economy. This does not mean the absence of opposition, as the battle over the North American Free Trade Agreement (NAFTA) in the United States or the backlash against the 1992 agenda in Europe both attest. But a basic commitment to the free flow of goods and capital (although not of labor) is fairly well institutionalized among the advanced industrial states, partly because important economic interests have stakes in an open economy and partly because compensatory mechanisms attenuate the social costs associated with an open economy.

In the developing world, by contrast, the domestic coalitions sup- portive of a more open stance toward the world economy have not usually been consolidated. Interventionist development strategies have naturally created strong interests in the policy status quo, and in many developing countries, deep intellectual divisions and political cleavages remain over the merits of closer integration with the world economy. Moreover, the institutional capacity of the governments of developing countries to buffer the effects of greater openness, or to manage the administrative demands associated with the deep integration agenda, is limited for fiscal and administrative reasons, especially in the low-income countries. During the 1980s and 1990s, political instability and the daunting challenges of consolidating new democratic systems only complicated the prospects for overcoming these hurdles.

These skeptical expectations are partly justified. The 1980s and 1990s have been a period of unprecedented economic reform, an undeniable turning point in the economic history of the developing world. However, most of the reform efforts have centered on policy

7. For a review of the developing countries' integration into the GATT system, see OECD (1992).

areas that are not related to the deep integration agenda: balance of payments, macroeconomic policy, and exchange rate adjustments; "shallow" integration efforts such as trade reform; or domestic policy changes such as privatization or the removal of subsidies and price controls that may have international repercussions but do not seem to be the result of international policy coordination. Discussions of deep integration in the developing world are clearly less far along than they are among the advanced industrial states.

Nonetheless, issues of deep integration are becoming more salient for several advanced developing countries. Not only are traditional at-the-border barriers falling, but governments are *unilaterally* emulating the standards, laws, and practices of the developed countries and aligning domestic practice with international norms. They are also participating actively in a complex and overlapping web of bilateral, regional, and multilateral initiatives, many of which include deep integration issues.

The standard explanation for the push toward deeper integration among the advanced industrial states begins with the observation that traditional barriers to trade and investment have fallen substantially, and economic interdependence has increased. The reduction of at-the-border barriers makes the discriminatory effect of remaining regulatory differences more significant and creates strong incentives to expand the scope of international cooperation.[8]

This argument is plausible among countries of roughly equal power and status, where domestic political alignments are broadly favorable to international cooperation, and where existing regulatory arrangements have already converged to a great extent; the European Community provides the model. However, these conditions do not generally apply to relations between the developed and developing world.

In this book I maintain that the willingness of developing countries to entertain the deep integration agenda can only be understood in

---

8. See, for example, Lawrence (forthcoming). Aaron and others (1993) distinguish between problems of arbitrage and spillovers, which result from regulatory differences. Arbitrage refers to economic advantages that accrue to one state by maintaining a regulatory stance that is different from that of its trading partners; an example would be lax financial or environmental regulation. Spillovers refer to any effects that the regulatory policies of one country may have on other nations. This logic is similar to a long line of theorizing on regional integration among political scientists; for an early review that is still applicable, see Keohane and Nye (1975).

light of powerful external economic and political constraints that operated on them during the 1980s.[9] The international constraints on developing countries took four interrelated forms. First, the profound economic problems arising from external debt produced strong incentives for policy change, especially so that developing countries could regain access to foreign investment and borrowing. In several countries, crises also affected domestic politics by strengthening the hand of "internationalist" forces inside and outside the government. These economic and political changes increased the willingness of governments to align domestic policy with international norms, especially in areas such as intellectual property protection that directly affect the perceptions and behavior of investors.

With both commercial lending and foreign direct investment in retreat, the relative importance of the International Financial Institutions (IFIs) and bilateral donors increased; their lending policies constituted a second external constraint on the governments of developing countries. IFI lending had always been conditional on the pursuit of policy reform, but the conception of conditionality widened dramatically during the 1980s. Bilateral assistance from the advanced industrial states was also based on a new concern with domestic policy reform. The policy norms embodied in conditional lending thus became an important point of reference for reform efforts in developing countries. In effect, conditionality became a route to deeper integration.

A third source of pressure on the developing countries arose from the commercial policies of the advanced industrial states, especially the United States. Growing corporate interest in exports and investment opportunities in the developing countries resulted in U.S. trade policy, shifting toward an emphasis on opening foreign markets. The threat of sanctions became an instrument not only for reducing traditional trade barriers but also for forcing broader regulatory changes favorable to American firms. Additional pressures arose from regional arrangements, particularly NAFTA, which set high standards for the future participation of developing countries. As with the imposition of conditionality, such trade pressures were not uniformly successful in inducing policy changes in developing countries, but given the vulnerability of the targeted countries, bilateralism proved surprisingly effective.

9. For a similar argument, see Stallings (1992).

Closely related to these bilateral actions was a fourth set of pressures on developing country governments: changes in the international regime governing world trade and investment. Not only did the industrial states increasingly reject the claims of advanced developing countries to preferential treatment, but they were also willing to abrogate the principle of nondiscrimination in favor of "conditional" most favored nation (MFN) status: the principle that countries could not benefit from international agreements without offering reciprocal concessions. Conditional MFN was used to enforce compliance on new issues such as intellectual property protection, which were key components of the deep integration agenda, and the advanced developing countries were among its main targets.

Comparative Politics

These four external pressures did not operate evenly across the developing world nor did they translate uniformly into a willingness to entertain the deep integration agenda. To understand these national variations, a comparative analysis of the political and economic differences among developing countries is needed.[10]

Developing countries might be grouped in many ways for such analysis. Level of development is the most obvious. The deep integration agenda is clearly more salient to the advanced developing countries than to the poorer ones; for that reason, this book emphasizes the newly industrializing countries (NICs) of East and Southeast Asia and Latin America.

There is some justification for surveying the developing world by region, however. There are similarities in the level of economic development, policy problems, and even political structures within regions. More important, the external economic and political environment also varies with geography, as do the possibilities for regional integration arrangements. The regional political context helps determine the organizational form that deep integration efforts will take.

10. The literature on the comparative political economy of adjustment is vast, but projects that attempt cross-regional comparisons from different perspectives include Nelson (1990); Haggard and Kaufman (1992); Bates and Krueger (1993); Bresser and others, (1993); Williamson (1993) and Haggard and Webb (1994).

The East and Southeast Asian developing countries include the East Asian newly industrializing countries—Korea, Taiwan, Singapore, and Hong Kong—and the large countries in the Association of Southeast Asian Nations (ASEAN)—Indonesia, Malaysia, Thailand, and the Philippines. Though these countries differ in income levels and domestic politics, they also share some important similarities with respect to the deep integration agenda. The four "original" NICs have been the most successful developing country exporters of manufactures. Except for the Philippines, the major Southeast Asian countries are now following a similar export-oriented development trajectory, assisted in the late-1980s by a large infusion of Japanese foreign direct investment.

Precisely because of their export success, the East and Southeast Asian developing countries have faced important conflicts with their major trading partners, particularly the United States. Initially, these conflicts resulted in straightforward protectionist responses, usually in the form of orderly marketing agreements and voluntary export restraints. During the 1980s, however, trade policy conflicts shifted toward greater emphasis on unfair trade practices, measures to open markets, and regulatory reform in the NICs themselves.

The international political economy of deep integration in the East and Southeast Asian countries thus centers largely on the management of external political pressures from trading partners. As with all "integration under pressure," domestic sources of resistance emerge: in East and Southeast Asia, these include not only weak and protected sectors that have been the beneficiaries of closed markets, but governments that have relied on various forms of intervention for industrial policy purposes and to cement bases of political support.

Several domestic political features of the East and Southeast Asian countries have made them relatively amenable to deeper integration, however. First, rapid growth and increasing internationalization have produced domestic political forces that are sensitive to external sanctions or independently interested in the advantages of closer integration with the advanced industrial states. Second, strong governments have initiated and sustained reform measures throughout the region. This was true in earlier periods, when export-oriented reforms were initially launched under authoritarian auspices, and in the more incremental reforms of the past decade.

The second cluster of important developing countries is in Latin America; I consider primarily Mexico and the larger South American countries that experienced debt crises in the 1980s. In these countries, crises were instrumental in forcing reforms, which were centered at first on stabilizing prices and the balance of payments. Yet the recent wave of reform resulted in surprisingly aggressive governmental attacks on traditional at-the-border trade and investment barriers, a process of privatization of state-owned enterprises, and important regulatory reforms.

Why were reform efforts in Latin America so wide ranging? To a certain extent, the logic was similar to that which operated in the East and Southeast Asian countries. The larger Latin American NICs had become successful exporters of manufactures, had maintained relatively protectionist regimes, and as a result had become increasingly vulnerable to bilateral pressure from the United States.

Yet crises also affected policy reform in two further ways. To solve severe balance of payments problems Latin America put a premium on attracting foreign investment. The international financial institutions also gained a larger role than had been true in the past. Liberalization, privatization, and regulatory reform were often undertaken with support from the international financial institutions and were explicitly designed both to secure investment in the short run and to signal government intentions toward foreign investment in the future.

Even more important, the economic crisis discredited inward-looking development models and enabled reformist leaderships to initiate wide-ranging economic reforms; by the early 1990s virtually all of the Latin American countries had launched packages of economic reforms that included both shallow and deep integration measures. The chief question for the next decade is whether these reforms will be consolidated or reversed, and that will hinge mostly on differences in domestic institutions and coalitions.

In Asia, outward-oriented economic reforms were generally launched under authoritarian or dominant party auspices; in Korea, Taiwan, and Singapore, these reforms date to the 1960s. As a result, these policies had yielded fruit and created constituencies with a strong stake in global markets. Even where political liberalization occurred—in Korea, Taiwan, and to a lesser extent Thailand—this political change took place against a backdrop of relatively robust economic performance and increasingly outward-oriented economies and did not result in fundamental challenges to the existing policy course.

In the Latin American countries, by contrast, extremely difficult challenges of stabilization and structural adjustment overlapped with democratic transitions or political liberalization; in some cases, political change could be traced directly to economic crisis. These policy reforms meant more or less frontal assaults on the interests of well-entrenched groups rooted in long-standing import-substitution policies; though internationalization had increased steadily over time, Latin American countries' involvement in the international trading system was substantially less than in East and Southeast Asia. Moreover, the reform efforts took place in much less auspicious economic circumstances and were therefore far more likely to generate opposition.

This dual process of economic and political liberalization was managed relatively smoothly in Chile, where reforms had been initiated by the authoritarian Pinochet government. In Mexico, the ruling party retained its hold on power despite poor economic performance and was also capable of launching dramatic economic reforms. Not coincidentally, these two countries represent the "early reformers" in the hemisphere.

In several other countries, democratic transitions or political delays in adjustment contributed to further economic deterioration before new reform initiatives were launched in the late 1980s or early 1990s; this was true in Brazil, Argentina, Peru, Bolivia, Colombia, and Venezuela. The outstanding question for recent reforms in all of these countries is whether they will generate adequate economic returns to become politically consolidated. The policy reversals in Venezuela in the early 1990s suggests that the answer is far from certain.

Because of their higher level of development, the deep integration agenda has been most relevant to the middle-income countries of Asia and Latin America. However India, the Mediterranean associates of the European Community, and the lower-income countries of the African-Caribbean-Pacific (ACP) grouping deserve some consideration as well.

Although India avoided the debt crisis, it confronted many structural problems in the 1980s stemming from its long-standing strategy of statism and import substitution. Fiscal problems, in particular, were an important impetus for the policy reforms of the early 1990s. External pressures also affected reforms. India had a closed trade

regime and relatively restrictive rules governing foreign direct investment, yet increasingly sought to expand its export of manufactured
goods. This policy stance naturally generated conflicts with trading
partners, particularly the United States. India has also been forced to
rely more heavily on conditional lending from the IFIs than it has in
the past. Despite India's low per capita income, its technological base,
export potential, and size have forced the government to consider
several deep integration issues.[11]

Finally, a politically diverse category of developing countries is
made up largely of Africa and several of the Maghreb and Middle
Eastern countries.[12] Some of these countries, particularly Turkey and
the Maghreb (Morocco, Algeria, and Tunisia), were at a much higher
level of development than their sub-Saharan African counterparts
and experienced adjustment difficulties similar to those undergone in
Latin America. Turkey, for example, undertook dramatic economic
reforms in the early 1980s with strong support from the IFIs, at the
same time that it was also undergoing a transition back to democratic
rule; as with the Latin American countries, deep integration issues did
arise during the reform, especially given Turkey's interest in accession
to the European Community.

The performance of the sub-Saharan African economies during
the 1980s was highly variable, but virtually all suffered big setbacks.
Given their lower level of development, lack of substantial industrial
or manufacturing base, dependence on export of raw materials, and
perhaps most important, their relative economic unimportance to the
advanced industrial states, issues of deep integration have not been
salient. However, the extremely heavy reliance of these economies on
multilateral and bilateral aid did subject them to greater external
policy scrutiny from the IFIs and from the European Community.

International Institutions

What organizational form will the deep integration in the developing countries take? Whether the developing countries will orient

11. I omit from consideration Pakistan, Sri Lanka, and Bangladesh.
12. I omit from consideration the oil exporters, which faced distinctive problems that
go beyond the interests of this study.

themselves primarily toward the multilateral institutions, particularly the World Trade Organization, or whether they will gravitate toward regional arrangements remains a central controversy for the trading system.[13]

The increasing demands on the developing countries to participate more fully in the multilateral institutions have already been noted, including their unprecedented participation in the Uruguay Round. Regional initiatives may also affect the deeper integration of some developing countries, though there are interesting variations across regions. In the Western Hemisphere, the North American Free Trade Agreement is the most ambitious effort to link a developing economy, Mexico, with two more advanced ones, and goes far beyond the traditional trade and investment agenda toward the harmonization of national policies that is the hallmark of deeper integration. Moreover, NAFTA is now considered a model that might be extended into a Western Hemisphere Free Trade Area, or at least is seen as a baseline for what will be expected of other developing countries in the region.

Elsewhere, regional arrangements have a less ambitious agenda for deep integration. For many reasons, regional institutions in the Pacific have historically been weak, though the Asia-Pacific Economic Co-operation initiative is now becoming the organizational focus for a discussion of deep integration questions. Europe maintains extensive and well-institutionalized relations with several developing countries in the Mediterranean, Africa, the Caribbean, and Asia, but there are few signs that these relations are evolving into deep integration agreements.

I conclude this study by arguing that the emphasis given to multi-lateral and regional arrangements should not overlook the vitality of bilateralism as a means of governing international trade and invest-ment relations, especially for the weaker developing countries.

Possibly, the new bilateralism is a route toward open regionalism or multilateralism. This would be true if bilateral pressure spurred liber-alization that was nondiscriminatory in nature and forced conver-gence around multilateral norms. For the most part, this response seems to be the case, but two signs of potential trouble are visible. First, the evidence shows some bilateral arrangements result in pref-erential, or what I call quasi-preferential, arrangements: agreements in which liberalization or harmonization is formally undertaken in a

13. See Lawrence (forthcoming); Bhagwati (1993).

nondiscriminatory way, but in which the content and design of the policy reveal an effort to favor the interests of one party over others.

Second, evidence is mounting that the scope of bilateralism is expanding in a highly intrusive fashion, encompassing new areas such as environmental and labor standards, "governance," and human rights and democracy. In these new areas, stringent and sometimes unrealistic standards have on occasion been set for developing countries. Moreover, advocates of this new conditionality in the advanced industrial states often find themselves allied with straightforward protectionists; the coalition of labor and environmental groups during the NAFTA debate in the United States is an example. If the new, expanded deep integration agenda is enforced through sanctions, it could easily be detrimental to the welfare of the developing countries.

Chapter 2

The International Setting

FOR many developing countries, the 1980s proved a very difficult decade. The problems were, first of all, economic. The heavily indebted countries, in particular, faced a swift decline in the availability of international commercial lending early in the decade and strong pressures to adjust as a result. Yet these economic constraints also coincided with three political developments: an expanding definition of conditionality for both multilateral and bilateral assistance; growing bilateral pressure on trade policy from the United States; and important changes in expectations for the developing countries' participation in the General Agreement on Tariffs and Trade (GATT).

The Economic Setting: Crisis and Policy Change

Sluggish and erratic growth in the advanced industrial states, matched by sharp fluctuations in import demand, contributed to the economic difficulties of the less developed countries (LDCs), especially in the early 1980s, and again in the early 1990s. Developments in the terms of trade were also inauspicious. Countries heavily dependent on commodity exports, especially oil exporters, experienced severe difficulties in the middle of the 1980s. However, the deterioration was more general; even the diversified export-oriented newly industrializing economies of East and Southeast Asia did poorly in this regard. All regions except Europe experienced stagnating export growth during the global recession in the early 1980s and again in 1985–86. After 1987, export growth resumed. Asia's trade growth was

15

especially robust, but the Western Hemisphere showed important signs of recovery too (table 2-1).

Developments in international financial markets were also adverse. High interest rates in the first three years of the 1980s increased the cost of servicing external obligations, led to a sharp increase in debt-service ratios, and contributed to the debt crisis. The most difficult adjustment for the debtors in the 1980s, however, was the sharp contraction of commercial lending that occurred after the Mexican crisis of August 1982. This adjustment is reflected in table 2-2 in the data on net transfers, which also demonstrate once again the differential effects of international developments across regions.[1] For Latin America as a whole, net transfers became negative in 1983 and remained that way into the 1990s. For East Asia, net transfers turned negative briefly in 1986, but the amounts were smaller and the development proved temporary. For Africa, net transfers to private creditors turned negative in 1983, but the dependence on commercial lending was less pronounced, and this development was offset by continued official flows. The Middle East and South Asia experienced fewer difficulties, although as will be seen in chapter 5, India faced balance of payments problems in the early 1990s.

Changes in the terms of trade, export performance, and the availability of foreign financing precipitated several short-term policy changes. The need to reverse current account deficits forced real exchange rate adjustments; the 1980s saw dramatic devaluations and changes in exchange rate regimes in the developing world.[2] The withdrawal of foreign lending also contributed to the need for macroeconomic policy adjustments: efforts to cut real government expenditure, raise revenues, restrain the growth of wages, and control the growth of the money supply, usually through, or with the effect of, raising real interest rates.

Why external shocks and corresponding macroeconomic policy adjustments might also be associated with trade and investment liberalization and the reforms associated with the deep integration agenda

1. Net transfers are obtained by subtracting interest payments on long-term and short-term debt and dividends on foreign direct investments from the aggregate net resource flows, or disbursements minus repayment of principal.

2. There is a clear link between the retrenchment of foreign lending, depreciation, and the trend toward more flexible exchange rate regimes. See International Monetary Fund (1989, pp. 7–8); Quirk and others (1987).

Table 2-1. *OECD Economic and Import Growth and Terms-of-Trade Indexes, 1980–92*

Item	1980	1981	1982	1983	1984	1985	1986	1987	1988	1989	1990	1991	1992
OECD economic growth[a]	0.9	1.3	-0.1	2.6	4.5	3.2	2.7	3.2	4.4	3.2	2.2	0.4	1.4
Growth in OECD imports[b]	19.9	-5.1	-6.1	-1.8	9.3	2.6	12.7	18.2	13.0	8.3	14.9	0.8	4.3
Terms-of-trade index[c]													
Developed market economies	100	98	100	101	100	101	110	111	113	112	111	111	113
Developing countries (DCs)	100	109	104	98	98	96	71	75	71	74	77	74	72
Western Hemisphere	100	100	94	92	93	91	77	76	74	75	76	72	69
Africa	100	109	103	95	96	95	63	67	59	64	71	66	63
North	100	116	109	99	99	99	56	63	54	61	72	67	65
Others	100	103	97	91	94	92	72	71	65	67	70	65	62
Asia	100	113	111	102	103	99	68	76	71	73	78	74	73
West	100	120	120	106	107	104	52	61	49	57	68	61	59
South and Southeast	100	101	97	96	98	94	86	88	90	87	85	84	83

a. OECD economic growth is calculated from the indexes of GDP growth of countries at constant prices. See IMF (1993).

b. Growth in OECD imports is percentage change.

c. See appendix A for country groupings for the terms-of-trade index.

Table 2-2. *Developing Countries' Export Growth and Net Transfers, 1980–92*

Item	1980	1981	1982	1983	1984	1985	1986	1987	1988	1989	1990	1991	1992
LDC export growth[a]	34.3	-1.2	-12.5	-7.1	5.0	-5.4	-7.7	20.4	13.9	12.6	13.3	...	...
Western Hemisphere	30.1	7.0	-9.9	0.1	7.1	-7.1	-15.9	11.9	12.5	10.2	8.6	...	...
Africa	37.1	-20.0	-12.7	-8.1	3.5	-2.5	-21.0	10.8	-1.2	8.5	27.3	...	...
Asia	34.5	1.1	-13.5	-9.4	4.5	-5.7	-1.8	25.3	17.0	14.2	13.6	...	...
Europe	17.2	0.9	4.3	4.1	3.5	-4.3	9.7	8.0	4.4	-7.8	-8.1	...	...
World interest rate[b]	13.4	16.1	13.7	10.1	11.8	9.1	6.9	7.6	8.4	9.3	8.5	6.3	4.2
Net transfers to DCs[c]	19.6	...	6.4	-2.4	-21.9	-36.2	-35.7	-25.1	-40.9	-28.4	-12.7	-8.5	13.1
Africa	5.3	...	6.2	4.0	0.5	-2.0	-1.3	2.9	-1.3	0.0	-1.5	-6.1	-3.9
East Asia and Pacific	3.7	...	1.5	4.4	-0.1	-1.9	-8.1	-11.4	-7.4	-4.5	8.2	12.9	16.0
Europe and the Mediterranean	7.0	...	-1.5	-1.5	-5.0	-3.2	-6.0	-1.6	-9.0	1.6	-7.6	-2.9	12.6
Latin America and the Caribbean	-1.5	...	-6.2	-12.4	-18.7	-30.6	-26.4	-19.8	-25.7	-27.6	-4.9	-10.2	-8.3
North Africa/Mideast	1.7	...	1.4	0.5	-0.3	0.2	4.4	3.4	-0.2	0.1	-9.2	-4.2	-4.3
South Asia	3.4	...	5.2	2.6	1.7	1.4	1.7	1.5	2.6	2.0	2.4	1.9	1.0

a. LDC export growth is percentage change. See appendix A for country groupings.

b. World interest rates are the one-year London Interbank offer rate on U.S. dollar deposits. See IMF (1993, p. 94).

c. Net transfers to developing countries refers to billions of U.S. dollars and are net flows minus interest payments (or disbursements minus total debt payments). The 1980–85 data are from World Bank (1990); 1986–92 data are from World Bank (1993).

is puzzling.[3] In the 1930s, balance of payments and debt crises spurred the substitution of imports, particularly in the larger developing countries such as India, Turkey, Brazil, Argentina, and Mexico and gave rise to a more autarkic and interventionist policy stance. In the 1980s, by contrast, an inward-looking policy course seemed foreclosed. The reasons are multiple and have to do with the profound structural changes in the advanced developing countries connected with their rapid industrialization in the post World War II period. The opportunities for continued import substitution were limited, and ties to the world economy had become more varied, complex, and difficult to sever.

One consequence of the crisis was the incentive it created to attract foreign investment, especially foreign direct investment.[4] During the borrowing boom of the 1970s, the middle-income developing countries could depend on fairly easy access to external financing through the Eurocurrency markets. The relative weight of foreign direct investment in total capital flows declined, and rules governing foreign investment became more selective and restrictive. With the evaporation of international commercial lending, severe balance of payments constraints, and declining domestic investment, governments became highly sensitive to the interests of foreign creditors and investors.

Besides the measures required to reestablish macroeconomic stability, the efforts to attract investment included several policy changes. First, crises spurred "shallow integration" reforms of the investment regime: lifting of sectoral and equity restrictions on foreign investment, eliminating various performance requirements, liberalizing the rules governing the repatriation of capital, profits, and dividends, and even liberalizing the capital account. More generally, efforts arose to move the rules governing foreign investment in the direction of national treatment, that is, reducing or eliminating differential treatment of foreign and domestic firms.

Efforts to attract investment spilled over into the deep integration agenda in several ways, however. Intellectual property rights is the clearest example of a deep integration policy area in which domestic laws are brought into conformity with international standards to attract or appease investors. But the pressure to align the domestic regulatory climate to international norms has been much broader. As

3. See Rodrik (1994).
4. See IMF (1992, pp. 26–27, 29–31).

the countries in Latin America demonstrate, one effect of the crisis of the 1980s was to spawn new privatization efforts; privatization, in turn, was typically accompanied by reforms of the regulatory structure in the affected industries. Similarly, reforms in the financial sector or with respect to commercial law cannot be understood simply in terms of deregulation; rather, regulatory reform or reregulation is occurring. Existing international norms, the practices of the advanced industrial states, and the interests of foreign investors exercise a strong influence on what governments do.

Developing countries often undertook these reforms unilaterally. However, they had strong reasons to embed them in multilateral, regional, or bilateral agreements when possible. Politicians undertaking reform face an obvious problem in establishing their credibility with investors because reform measures are reversible and reputation emerges only over time.[5] One way for governments to signal intentions and provide assurances is by enacting institutional changes that increase the cost of policy reversal. Delegation to government agencies that are insulated from short-term political manipulation, and which thus enjoy the confidence of the international financial institutions, creditors, and investors, is one mechanism for accomplishing this objective. Sylvia Maxfield, for example, finds a widespread trend in the 1980s and early 1990s toward the strengthening of central banks in developing countries.[6] International agreements that raise the cost of policy reversal also signal government intent and tie the hands of successor governments. The numerous deep integration provisions of the North American Free Trade Agreement (NAFTA) had precisely this objective.

Expanding Conditionality

Adverse economic circumstances and declining foreign investment and lending were not the only features of the international environment to impinge on the policy choices of the developing countries. The influence of the international financial institutions also increased as a result of the crisis.[7] With few exceptions, the rescheduling of

5. Rodrik (1989).
6. Maxfield (1993, chap. 3).
7. For an overview, see Kahler (1990).

commercial and public debt has been contingent on the negotiation of high-conditionality, upper-tranche programs with the International Monetary Fund (IMF), usually supported by World Bank and regional development bank lending. The debt crisis also led to substantive changes in the "conditionality norm": the presumption that multilateral and bilateral financial assistance is granted contingent on policy adjustments by the recipients. These adjustments included both shallow and deep integration measures. The influence of the international financial institutions and major donors should not be exaggerated and is in any case difficult to disentangle from the underlying economic difficulties to which conditional lending is a response. However, conditionality did help establish and transmit international policy norms and therefore must be considered a factor in the increasing integration of the developing countries into the world economy in the past decade.

The conditionality norm evolved during the 1980s. In the immediate aftermath of the Mexican debt crisis of August 1982, conditionality was geared largely toward restoring balance of payments equilibrium. By the mid-1980s, however, perceptions began to shift. The Baker Plan, unveiled at the IMF meetings in Seoul in September 1985, recognized that the difficulties facing the debtors were longer term and structural in nature and promised that international financial institutions would increase their lending; the plan emphasized increasing the World Bank's role. The World Bank initiated structural adjustment lending in 1979; the volume of this rapidly disbursing, policy-based lending grew dramatically in the mid-1980s. The IMF's Extended Fund Facility and Structural Adjustment Facility were based on similar premises and allowed for longer programs than the traditional standbys. The Baker Plan was explicit, however, that structural adjustment programs were the quid pro quo for increased assistance.

By 1988 it was clear that the Baker Plan was inadequate,[8] and in March 1989, U.S. Treasury Secretary Nicholas Brady announced that the United States would support debt reduction. Conditionality re-

8. In particular, the "plan" had no way of inducing new lending from the commercial banks, and an increasing number of countries even halted repayment to the international financial institutions and went into arrears. An assessment by the World Bank of the Baker Plan is worth quoting at some length: "Per capita income in the Baker Plan 17 countries, which were lower in 1985 than in 1982, declined further between 1985 and 1988. Despite large trade surpluses, the Baker 17 countries' total debt continued to rise in relation to

mained central to the debt reduction strategy, however, and became even more significant given that an increasing number of countries were undertaking IMF and World Bank programs simultaneously and were thus subject to implicit or explicit cross conditionality.[9] As Miles Kahler summarizes, the underlying bargain remained constant over the entire decade: "stringent adjustment for a modest amount of financing."[10]

The combination of increased multilateral lending and the evaporation of commercial credit placed the IMF and the World Bank in a strategic position to define the policy reform agenda. The menu of structural adjustment measures called for by the IMF and World Bank fell into three broad categories: expenditure-reducing policies; expenditure-switching policies; and supply-side policies designed to remove the structural causes of macroeconomic imbalances, increase the efficiency of resource use, and increase savings and investment. The first two sets of measures require no comment, except to note that the effort to switch production from nontradables to tradables through adjustments of the real exchange rate is itself a key precondition for greater integration with the world economy.

Of greater interest is that 84 percent of all conditions contained in loan agreements fell into the third category of supply-side measures.[11] The most common was trade policy reform; nearly 80 percent of all loans demanded action in this area. Sectoral policies also became an increasingly common component of structural adjustment lending, however, and in three areas overlapped substantially with the deep integration agenda: industry, finance, and reform of the state-owned enterprise sector. In all three cases, regulatory reform or the establishment of altogether new regulatory structures was the norm. For example, a World Bank study notes that policy reform for the industrial sector "has shifted from restructuring and incentives for direct

exports up to 1986. Their total debt service ratio improved modestly . . . [but] the real depreciation of the currencies of the Baker countries, often necessary to generate the external resource transfer, further increased the level of external debt relative to domestic output over this period." World Bank (1990, p. 13).

9. Similarly, those low-income countries eligible for forgiveness and concessional rescheduling of official bilateral debt under the so-called Toronto terms or for access to the World Bank's debt reduction facility for low-income countries were expected to have IMF- or World Bank-supported adjustment programs in place.

10. Kahler (1990, p. 47).

11. Webb and Shariff (1992, pp. 69–70, table 5–1).

investment toward pricing policy, entry barriers, the regulatory environment and technology policy"; in effect, lending to the industry sector supported reform of competition policy.[12] Financial sector loans are also an important area where liberalization measures have taken place along with substantial regulatory reform. Regulatory reform, including the development of new rules for foreign investors and competition policy, is also a crucial element in the reform of state-owned enterprises and privatization.

A variety of policy measures fall into the category of structural adjustment. Despite the views of critics, there is no single template for structural adjustment lending. Nonetheless, both the IMF and World Bank base structural adjustment lending on the belief that developing countries can benefit from greater openness to trade and investment; the Bank and the Fund are therefore big champions of shallow integration. The sector-specific policy recommendations that are an important component of World Bank lending are also based on explicit or implicit views of the appropriate policy and regulatory regime, and thus at least some policy convergence is implied. For the developing countries, harmonization may occur not only through negotiations with other governments but also through interactions with the multilateral financial institutions.

Donor countries have generally been content to leave issues of policy conditionality in the hands of the international financial institutions.[13] During the 1980s, however, a growing recognition took place that bilateral aid efforts and project assistance were unlikely to yield fruit if the policy framework was not appropriate. Political considerations for important clients did sometimes weaken donor commitment to conditionality and may have even undermined the efforts of the multilateral institutions in some instances. Nonetheless, the general tendency during the 1980s was for the major donors to expand their scrutiny of aid recipients' overall

12. See Webb and Shariff (1992, p. 78).

13. One important exception to this is the consultative groups (CGs) sponsored by the World Bank, which constitute one mechanism through which bilateral aid is coordinated and donors gain the opportunity to scrutinize the country's overall policy framework. Since the first one was established in 1958, forty countries, mostly low-income ones, have had one or more of these aid group meetings. In the 1980s the frequency of CG meetings increased and the number of countries with CGs grew. See Krueger, Michalopoulos, and Ruttan (1989, p. 106–07).

policy framework, thus buttressing the efforts of the international financial institutions (IFIs).

The U.S. aid program is divided into three major instruments: economic support funds, which go to politically important clients; food aid; and development assistance, which goes to support economic and social development through funding of projects. The U.S. aid machinery has long been criticized for the conflict between political and economic objectives in aid policy, the intrusive involvement of Congress in detailing spending priorities, and the unwieldy focus on personnel-intensive projects.[14] However, under the Reagan and Bush administrations, the government did attempt to expand the criteria for aid policy to include a consideration of the overall policy framework. More important, the United States strongly champions the IFIs as guardians of conditionality.

As will be shown in more detail in chapter 5, European Community (EC) aid policy has also undergone a shift toward greater conditionality. Lomé IV (1990), the most recent agreement between the European Community and its developing country associates, earmarked a share of aid funds for structural adjustment (rather than project) purposes and contained a services chapter and an explicit commitment to the development of the private sector, including improved protection for foreign investment. Parallel trends were visible after 1989 in EC policy toward the Mediterranean associates.[15]

Although the aid policies of the individual European countries vary in their geographic and programmatic emphases, a trend toward greater concern with overall policy is visible.[16] At the Franco-African summit in La Baule in June 1990, France made clear that its assistance would increasingly be conditional on economic and political reform. The share of program assistance in Britain's total aid increased during the 1980s, largely as a result of increased assistance to sub-Saharan Africa in support of World Bank and IMF structural adjustment lending. In 1987 Germany initiated a cofinancing facility to support structural adjustment lending.

14. See Zimmerman (1993); Krueger (1992).
15. See Cosgrove and Laurent (1992, pp. 127–33); Grilli (1993, pp. 213–14).
16. See, for example, the policy statement by the OECD Development Assistance Committee Aid Ministers and Heads of Aid Agencies (OECD 1989, i–vi). See also Lumsdaine (1993, pp. 104–36); OECD (1991).

Japan's aid policy deserves special mention. On the one hand, it conforms with the trend toward "policy dialogue" between donors and recipients. In the 1990 white paper on overseas development assistance, and in a major policy speech by Prime Minister Kaifu in April 1991, the Japanese government signaled a shift in policy by suggesting that aid could be conditioned on limits on military spending, progress toward democratization, and the adoption of appropriate development policies.[17]

Several analyses of Japan's overseas development assistance have noted that it is strongly motivated by economic considerations. "Appropriate" development policies include, above all, an open and cooperative stance toward foreign direct investment in general, and Japanese investment in particular.[18]

The picture is complicated because Japan has been more and more aggressive in advancing its conception of development, which is at least somewhat at odds with the general direction of the policy conditionality of the IFIs. Japan's 1991 policy statement, as well as other government studies of international cooperation, have suggested that Japan's perception of the appropriate policy regime for developing countries is more interventionist than that advanced by the World Bank, especially regarding industrial policy.[19] A strong emphasis in Japan's aid policy on facilitating trade and investment, and its acceptance of a significant state role in conducting industrial policy, has been the basis for the claim that a new form of "deep" regional integration is emerging in East Asia centered on Japan.

Even if there has been a change toward more comprehensive conditionality by multilateral and bilateral donors, do countries actually comply? Systematic research in this area is methodologically difficult and limited. The World Bank's internal study, summarized in table 2-3, finds fairly high compliance. My study of Extended Fund Facility programs found that a large number were canceled for noncompliance.[20] Kahler surveys a sample of nineteen governments during the 1980s, using a broader criterion of compliance than the detailed coding of individual policy measures by the World Bank, but

17. See Unger (1993, p. 158); Rix (1993b, pp. 34–35).
18. See Unger (1993); Rix (1993a); Nester (1992); Koppel and Orr (1993); Ensign (1992).
19. Unger (1993, pp. 160–63).
20. Haggard (1986).

Table 2-3. *Content of World Bank Lending Operations and Compliance, Fiscal 1979–89*
Percent

Item	Share of loans requiring actions in the policy area	Fully implemented	At least substantially implemented
Absorption reduction			
Fiscal	67	74	82
Monetary	42	67	83
Switching policies			
Exchange rate	45	75	85
Wage policy	22	45	91
Supply-side policies			
Trade	79	62	85
Industry	44	72	92
Energy	27	69	80
Agriculture	62	62	81
Finance	51	73	89
Government	72	63	81
Public enterprise	65	66	80
Social policy	24	59	91
Other	49	. . .	. . .

Source: Webb and Shariff (1992, pp. 71–72, tables 5-2 and 5-3). The data on implementation refer to judgments about the extent to which the condition was fulfilled at the time of final tranche release.

one that is arguably more appropriate for gauging the overall progress of efforts by individual countries. He finds that only five of the nineteen countries surveyed had implemented sustained structural adjustment programs.[21] In an intensive study of nine countries receiving World Bank structural adjustment loans, Paul Mosely, Jane Harrigan, and John Toye also find that only two—Turkey and Thailand—actually met more than two-thirds of the conditions attached to structural adjustment and sectoral adjustment loans.[22] Yet even when slippage was pronounced, underestimating the significance of conditionality, especially for smaller countries, would be wrong. Shallow integration has been central to the agenda of the international

21. Kahler (1992).
22. Malawi, Ghana, the Philippines, and Jamaica implemented between 55 percent and 63 percent of the conditions, and Kenya, Guyana, and Ecuador had implementation rates of less than 38 percent. Mosely, Harrigan, and Toye (1992).

financial institutions, but questions of deep integration have also affected structural and sectoral adjustment programs.

Bilateralism and the Developing Countries

Escalating demands from advanced industrial countries were a third international constraint on developing countries in the 1980s. This phenomenon has been labeled reciprocity, unilateralism, and unrestricted bargaining, but I refer to it as bilateralism: the negotiation of agreements between two parties that are not subject to a mutually agreed set of international principles and rules and in which states are not limited in their recourse to sanctions to realize their objectives.[23]

To understand the role of bilateralism in the deeper integration of the developing countries, it is crucial to draw a distinction between traditional protection and contingent protection. The emergence of the newly industrializing countries was important in the resurgence of traditional protection in the United States and Europe.[24] The objective of such protection was straightforward: to shield American and European industries from low-price competitors through the imposition of quotas, voluntary export restraints, orderly marketing agreements, and sectoral accords. Such protection naturally affected LDC exports, but it did not have direct implications for the debates over shallow or deep integration.

Contingent protection, by contrast, is designed to deter particular "unfair" practices, and if necessary, change the behavior of the exporting country's firms and government through threat or imposition of sanctions. Protection is contingent on the behavior of the target. GATT rules on subsidies and dumping, which permit the imposition of countervailing duties and taxes, provide the most important example.[25] As with the widening of the conditionality agenda, however, the

23. For other treatments of the phenomenon, see Cline (1983); Bhagwati and Patrick (1990); Oye (1992).

24. Yoffie (1983).

25. In fact, there is evidence that the unfair trade laws have increasingly been turned to purely protectionist purposes. See Finger, Hall, and Nelson (1982); Destler (1992, pp. 139–72); Nivola (1993, chap. 4). Unfair trade actions have resulted in remedies that are discriminatory, are often the first step in the initiation of voluntary export restraints and

range of policies deemed unfair and thus subject to external scrutiny and sanction has broadened to include virtually the entire deep integration agenda. By the late 1980s, bilateralism had become the most significant route toward deeper integration for the advanced developing countries, though one that suggests that the process may be far from benign.

It is useful to begin with a discussion of the "traditional" unfair trade laws covering dumping and subsidies.[26] Though they are not typically considered a component of the deep integration agenda, these rules have significant consequences for the strategies that firms and governments in developing countries can legitimately pursue in their efforts to industrialize and expand their exports of manufactures. Rules governing subsidies go to the heart of industrial and competition policies. As even the World Bank has recognized in its recent study of the East Asian miracle, export subsidies have been a component of the industrial strategies of the successful newly industrializing countries,[27] and differential pricing (in essence what dumping is) is arguably a reasonable business strategy for new market entrants. Advocates of an "activist" or "strategic" trade policy for the advanced industrial states explicitly affirm the need to use unfair trade laws to counter such industrial policies abroad.[28] Thus if the aggressive use of unfair trade policy instruments does not fit the typical model of deep integration around a new norm, it does imply what might be called negative convergence: a restriction of the range of industrial policy options that developing countries can pursue.

A study of the incidence of U.S. antidumping (ADs) and countervailing duty (CVDs) cases between 1980 and 1988 found that except for Brazil, developing countries were not unusually burdened by these actions, in the sense that their share of total cases over that period (37 percent) was almost exactly equal to their share of U.S. merchandise imports in 1987 (36 percent).[29] However, given that the number of

---

orderly marketing arrangements, and have an additional protectionist effect through the uncertainty they create for exporters and importers as the case is being investigated and prosecuted.

26. See Boltuck and Litan (1991); Nivola (1993).

27. World Bank (1993b); Amsden (1989).

28. Tyson (1992, pp. 267–74). These arguments are also exploited by protectionists who simply want to use unfair trade laws as a protectionist device, particularly by weakening the demand that injury be demonstrated.

29. Finger and Murray (1990, p. 9).

successful developing country exporters is small, the actions tend to focus on a handful of countries. Between 1980 and 1988, for example, 54 percent of all U.S. CVDs and ADs were lodged against four countries: Korea, Taiwan, Brazil, and Mexico. Cases against developing countries also led to restrictive outcomes somewhat more often than cases against developed countries—roughly three-quarters of the cases against developing versus two-thirds of the cases against developed countries—and were less than half as likely to be resolved through negotiated voluntary export restraints rather than by unilateral actions.[30] In the period 1989–92, the developing country share of all U.S. subsidy and antidumping actions increased to 55 percent.[31]

Though ADs and CVDs have been the most important "traditional" unfair trade policy instruments in the American arsenal, they are not the only ones. Section 301 will be discussed in more detail below, but mention must also be made of section 337 of the Tariff Act of 1930, the infamous Smoot-Hawley Act.[32] This section was dormant for nearly half a century, but procedural amendments introduced in the 1974 Trade Act made it more convenient to lodge complaints and brought the statute to life. The original section made broadly defined unfair trade practices unlawful but included provisions on trademark, patent, and copyright protection. The overwhelming majority of the more than 300 section 337 cases filed since 1974 concern intellectual property.[33] Of the outstanding exclusion orders in force under the section as of the end of 1992, most are directed against developing countries, particularly the East Asian newly industrializing countries. Of seventy-nine separate country citations, forty-six are against Korea, Taiwan, Hong Kong, and Singapore. As John Mutti argues, many of these cases involved labor-intensive products for which cost differentials no doubt constituted a chief motive for the action. Yet recently, Korea and Taiwan have been subject to actions

30. One reason for this suggested by Abreu and Fristch (1989, p. 121) is that unconditional most favored nation does not apply to the Subsidies Code; nonsignatories do not enjoy the benefit of an injury test.

31. Developing countries are defined to include China and the CIS states. Calculated from U.S. International Trade Commission (1990, pp. 187, 193, tables A-26, A-28); U.S. International Trade Commission (1991, pp. 207–08 and 213, tables A-19, A-21,); U.S. International Trade Commission (1992, pp. 199–201 and 207–08, tables A-19, A-21); U.S. International Trade Commission (1993, pp. 143–47 and 153–54, tables A-24 and A-26).

32. Mutti (1993).

33. See Dinan (1991).

against technologically sophisticated products, including semicon-
ductors, that have also been the focus of national industrial policies.[34]

need to stop

The United States is not the only advanced industrial state to use
unfair trade laws. CVDs have been used more sparingly by other
advanced industrial states, though Australia has used them extensively.[35] Australia, Canada, and the EU have employed antidumping
actions, however, and both the share of all dumping cases initiated
against developing countries and the share of positive findings against
less developed countries increased in the second half of the 1980s.[36]
In 1992 Australia reported the initiation of 123 antidumping actions
to GATT, 67 (55 percent) against developing countries. The EU
reported 51 antidumping actions in that year, 33 (65 percent) against
developing countries, and another 7 (14 percent) against the states of
the former Soviet Union.[37]

Bilateralism has by no means been limited to enforcing rules on
dumping and subsidies; to the contrary, the definition of what constitutes an unfair trade practice expanded dramatically in the 1980s,
especially in the United States. The crucial shift in U.S. trade policy can
be traced to the early years of the second Reagan administration.[38] In the
fall of 1985, trade policy pressures reached a new peak as a result of the
sharp increase in the U.S. trade deficit and the problems faced by both
export and import-competing industries from the strength of the dollar.
In Congress, strong political pressures for "solutions" to the trade
problem arose that were unabashedly protectionist.

The Reagan administration moved along several parallel fronts to
counter these pressures and preempt congressional action, in part by

34. Mutti (1993, p. 355); U.S. International Trade Commission (1993, pp. 157–60,
tables A-28, A-29).

35. See Winglee and others (1992, p. 120, table A12); U.S. International Trade Commission (1993, p. 131, table A-22).

36. Winglee and others (1992, p. 119, table A 11). It should also be noted, however,
that the developing countries are resorting to unfair trade actions. In 1992 Brazil and Chile
had recourse to CVDs and Brazil, Colombia, India, and Mexico reported ADs. U.S.
International Trade Commission (1993, pp. 131–42, tables A-22, A-23).

37. U.S. International Trade Commission (1993, pp. 133–42, table A-23).

38. Trade policy was not a central concern of the first Reagan administration, and the
trade policy record was decidedly mixed. The 1984 trade bill provided the authority to
launch a new round of multilateral trade talks, but the administration also undertook a
series of highly protectionist actions. These included the acceptance of Japanese auto
restraints in 1981, a tightening of textile quotas in 1983, and a global steel program that
called for the negotiation of restraint agreements with all major suppliers.

enlisting the support of anti-protectionist groups in American trade politics, firms whose foreign operations and trade ties give them an interest in open trade policies at home and abroad.[39] New urgency was given to securing European support for the launching of a new round of GATT negotiations, and the Plaza accord of September 22, 1985, initiated a new phase of international cooperation on exchange rates.

The day following the Plaza accord, President Reagan announced a new trade policy package that emphasized bilateral actions aimed at eliminating unfair trade practices abroad. In his speech, Reagan signaled that the United States would aggressively pursue dumping and subsidy cases, but he also announced three unfair trade investigations initiated by the administration: Korea's restrictions on the entry of American insurance firms; Brazil's restrictions on American computer exports that resulted from Brazilian industrial policy; and Japan's restrictions on cigarettes. As the choice of countries showed, the new program was clearly meant to force the pace of liberalization in developing countries.

The initiative also showed that the administration would take a more proactive stance toward unfair trade practices. Previously, investigations had been initiated at the behest of firms; now, the administration signaled its intention to launch investigations on its own. This proactive stance actually increased the influence of business on trade policy, however, since it created a new opportunity to lobby the U.S. Trade Representative both directly and through Congress on what the precise agenda of the new "proactive" stance should include.[40] Multinationals had long complained about restrictions on their operations; the emergence of strong pressures on trade policy provided the opportunity to link these complaints together under the rubric of trade-related investment measures (TRIMs). An emerging network of interested service industries, rooted in financial services and telecommunications, constituted an important component of the new market-opening bloc lobbying under the umbrella of the Coalition of Services Industries. The chemical and pharmaceutical industries had long complained about inadequate intellectual property protection in

---

39. Destler, Odell, and Elliott (1987); Milner (1988).

40. On the evolution of the new issues from a political economy standpoint, see Aggarwal (1992). On the specific issues, see Greenaway (1991) on trade-related investment measures, and Nogues (1990) and Mody (1990) on intellectual property rights.

the developing world, but in the 1980s, the broadcasting and recording industries and firms in the information and biotechnology fields also pressed the case for tougher protection, and intellectual property became a high priority of U.S. trade negotiators.

The Reagan administration's trade policy package implied that U.S. trade policy would move on two tracks. While pressing for negotiations in the GATT forum, the United States would also proceed bilaterally in areas in which there were no international rules, such as services, or in which existing conventions were deemed inadequate. Intellectual property fell into this second category. This intention meant that the United States had to develop some objectives to govern its bilateral negotiations. In a 1985 study, for example, the U.S. Trade Representative elaborated a set of principles affecting trade in services, including market access and the right to sell, national treatment, the principle that regulations should be the least restrictive possible, nondiscrimination, transparency, and elimination of subsidies. Similar broad principles were developed for intellectual property and announced in a policy statement in April 1986.[41]

The bilateral strategy naturally raised the issue of whether the United States was seeking preferences. In general, U.S. policy was to urge nondiscriminatory liberalization. Yet there was always the risk that countries might seek to blunt U.S. pressure by making concessions tailored to U.S. interests. This response might occur through overt preferences, or through what I have called quasi-preferential agreements: general rules that are formally nondiscriminatory but that effectively define the scope of their application in a preferential fashion.

The culmination of this new approach came with the passage of the Trade and Competitiveness Act of 1988, especially its amendments to section 301 of the 1974 Trade Act.[42] The initial 1974 301 legislation was designed to enforce trade rights conferred under GATT or bilateral treaties by giving the executive the right to initiate retaliatory action. For GATT-negotiated benefits, 301 complaints would initially be taken through GATT's dispute settlement machinery and were thus in principle consistent with GATT

---

41. See U.S. Trade Representative (1985a); Uphoff (1990, p. 1).
42. Bhagwati and Patrick (1990).

rules.[43] However, the original section 301 also contained a second category of punishable offenses: those that were found to be "unreasonable" barriers to U.S. trade but that were nonetheless not covered by GATT.

The expansion of this category of offenses in the 1988 act has been at the heart of the controversy over 301.[44] Under so-called Super 301 provisions, the U.S. Trade Representative was required to prepare an inventory of all foreign trade barriers, establish a priority list of countries singled out for action, set deadlines for compliance, and in the case that compliance was not forthcoming, retaliate. The 1988 act makes reference to barriers to trade in services and restrictions on foreign investment, and a separate provision of the bill, section 1374(a), targeted barriers in telecommunications. The so-called Special 301 provisions are similar but addressed to intellectual property rights. These provisions in the 1988 act thus provided further legal basis for the United States to pursue important elements of the deep integration component of the new GATT agenda on a bilateral basis.

However, the 1988 act went further, also making explicit mention of workers' rights, export targeting, and systematic toleration of anticompetitive practices. Export targeting became a hot topic before the passage of the 1984 Trade Act, though the administration succeeded in beating back efforts to include targeting provisions in that legislation. In the 1988 bill, however, targeting was included as an unfair trade practice and was defined permissively as any government actions that seek to increase the international competitiveness of an enterprise or industry. This is, of course, virtually a definition of industrial policy.[45]

The ability of the government to target anticompetitive practices by foreign firms was strengthened by the 1988 Trade Act both by general inclusion of anticompetitive practices as an unfair trade practice and by measures targeting several Japanese service industries; these latter provisions were the basis of a 301 case against Japan's construction industry. The ability to target competition policy received a further boost by a revision of antitrust law on April 3, 1992,

---

43. Though to be fully consistent with GATT, the panel would have to authorize 301 retaliation, which was never done for the six GATT-based cases brought under the pre-1988 Trade Act procedures. Bhagwati (1990, p. 2).

44. See Bello and Holmer (1990).

45. U.S. Trade Representative (1985); U.S. Department of Commerce (1985a).

which allowed the Justice Department to challenge foreign business conduct that harms American exports when the conduct would have violated U.S. antitrust laws if it took place in the United States. In effect, the United States had signaled its willingness to apply anti-trust law on an extraterritorial basis.[46] Given that antitrust provisions in the less developed countries are clearly less developed than in the advanced industrial states, LDCs were especially vulnerable to these provisions.

The expectation that the developing countries would become primary targets of these new trade policy instruments was con-firmed on June 16, 1989, when the U.S. Trade Representative identified its first Super 301 cases. Of six barriers to be prosecuted under Super 301, three concerned Japan, but the other three were aimed at Brazil and India, not coincidentally the two countries that had been most active in championing the third world in the Uru-guay negotiations.[47]

Table 2-4 contains data on all regular and Super 301 cases between 1985 and 1992, the period when U.S. policy moved toward bilateral market opening. Several findings are of interest. First, cases regarding developing countries during this period outnumber ones on devel-oped countries, a shift from the overall pattern of all 301 cases since 1974.[48] Second, the issues appear to be dominated by traditional import restrictions. One of the ten import restriction cases was di-rected at procedures. The remainder concerned agricultural products: beef, wine, and cigarettes.

Intellectual property issues are a close second, however. Intellec-tual property had first been linked to trade in the 1984 Trade Act in two distinct ways. First, failure to adequately protect intellectual property was deemed an unreasonable policy or practice, against which the president could take action under 301. Intellectual prop-erty protection was also included as a new criterion for renewal of privileges in the Generalized System of Preferences, highlighting U.S. concern with developing countries. With the 1988 trade bill, more pressure fell on countries providing inadequate protection. They were designated as Special 301 "priority watch list" and "watch list"

46. Finger and Fung (1993, pp. 22–24); Griffin (1992).
47. With Brazil the issue was import licensing. India was targeted for trade-related investment questions and barriers in services, particularly insurance.
48. See Finger (1993, p. 72, table 2).

Table 2-4. *U.S. 301 Cases against Developing Countries, 1985–92*

Type or outcome of case	Number of cases
By country	
Korea	5
India	4
Brazil	3
Taiwan	3
Thailand	3
Argentina	2
China	2
Indonesia	1
Total, developing countries	23
Total, developed countries	20
By dispute	
Import restrictions	10
Intellectual property	8
Services	2
Customs valuation	1
Investment	1
Export taxes	1
Disposition	
LDC makes concession and case terminated	12
U.S. threatens dispute resolution through GATT, LDC makes concession	2
Case goes to GATT dispute settlement	2
Initial discussions fail, U.S. makes further threat to retaliate, LDC makes concession	3
U.S. imposes sanctions, LDC makes concession	2
No merit to petition	1
Pending	1

Sources: U.S. International Trade Commission (1987, pp. 5-6–5-13; 1988, pp. 5-6–5-11; 1989, pp. 142–48; 1990, pp. 132–41; 1991, pp. 162–71; 1992, pp. 148–55; 1993, pp. 92–96).

nations.[49] Of the initial eight countries on the priority watch list, all were developing countries; of the seventeen on the watch list, all but four were. The government also initiated 301 investigations against China, India, and Thailand in 1991 for suspected violations of intellectual property.

49. At the same time that the first Super 301 cases were announced in 1989, the U.S. Trade Representative also reported under the Special 301 provisions. The U.S. Trade

Table 2-5. *USTR Designation of Developing Country Trade Barriers,*
Number of Countries Cited by Barrier, 1989–94

Type of barrier	1989	1990	1991	1992	1993	1994
Standards	6	6	6	6	6	9
Government procurement	6	9	9	10	10	13
Intellectual property	17	17	17	22	22	25
Service barriers	15	14	15	16	16	17
Investment barriers	13	12	12	16	16	16
Total[a]	57	58	59	70	70	80

Source: Calculated from U.S. Trade Representative (1989–94).

a. The total is of developing country citations. A number of developing countries are cited in more than one category, and four—Korea, Taiwan, Indonesia, and the members of the Gulf Cooperation Council—were cited for trade barriers in each of the five categories in 1994.

Virtually every 301 case resulted in policy changes in the direction that the United States sought. Designation as a priority watch list country also seemed to have some effect; within six months of the announcement, three of the eight countries—Korea, Taiwan, and Saudi Arabia—had taken policy actions on intellectual property protection that were deemed adequate to move them to the watch list, and one, Mexico, removed itself from Special 301 consideration altogether.[50]

After 1989, no new Super 301 priority countries were announced, though India was renamed in 1990. But this move did not mean that the bilateral strategy had been abandoned; rather, the high-profile approach that was a response to the political exigencies of the 1988 trade bill and its immediate aftermath gave way to bilateral consultations and negotiations, in part with efforts to secure concessions from the developing countries in the Uruguay Round.

The National Trade Estimate reports from 1989 through 1994 focus on various trade measures that are seen to constitute barriers to U.S. trade. Five are of greatest relevance to the deep integration agenda: standards, government procurement, intellectual property, service barriers, and investment barriers. Table 2-5 shows a steady expansion in the number of countries cited. Indeed, the only major

Representative concluded that no country met every standard for adequate and effective protection of intellectual property as advanced by the United States in the Tokyo Round, thus making "priority" designation meaningless; the priority watch list and watch list designations were designed to solve this problem.

50. U.S. International Trade Commission (1990, pp. 6, 136).

developing economy to avoid citation on at least one of these five issues was Hong Kong.

Similarly, the Department of the Treasury analyzes restrictions on the banking and securities sector. The *National Treatment Study* finds that most major developing countries maintain some barriers or regulatory practices injurious to American financial firms.[51] The most recent report, issued in 1990, examined Argentina, Brazil, India, Indonesia, Korea, the Philippines, Taiwan, Thailand, Turkey, and Venezuela. Of these countries, only Argentina, Indonesia, and Turkey had substantially met the national treatment standard, and even in these cases several complaints remained.

Bilateral efforts by the United States vis-à-vis the developing countries have also increasingly extended into more comprehensive reviews of the investment regime. After World War I, treaties of friendship, commerce, and navigation increasingly dealt with investment. A new round of these treaties was negotiated between 1946 and 1966, but the effort lost momentum when the developing countries became skeptical about the benefits of liberal foreign investment rules. In 1981 the United States emulated a growing European practice and began negotiating bilateral investment treaties (BITs). By 1990 the United States had concluded eight such treaties, all with developing countries, most of them relatively poor countries. The negotiation of the treaty itself most likely had some effect on changing investment rules.[52] Such treaties do not usually provide for completely free entry, but they do include efforts to make the conditions of entry simpler and more transparent, guarantee national and most favored nation treatment, facilitate financial transfers, and provide insurance against nationalization. They also provide for dispute settlement, typically by establishing that disputes will be submitted to the International Center for Settlement of Investment Disputes for resolution.[53]

Although the EC pioneered the BIT and has developed a growing network of "dialogues" with developing countries,[54] it has not used trade policy to pursue a strategy of market-opening bilateralism nearly

---

51. U.S. Department of the Treasury (1990).
52. Senegal, Zaire, Morocco, Turkey, Cameroon, Bangladesh, Egypt, and Grenada.
53. Salacluse (1990, pp. 664–73).
54. A number of these are conducted with regional counterparts such as the Association of Southeast Asian Nations, the Gulf Cooperation Council, and the Andean Pact. See Grilli (1993, chaps. 5–7).

as much as the United States has. In 1984 the Community adopted the "new commercial policy instrument," apparently modeled on U.S. section 301.[55] The procedure has been used sparingly, but one of the first cases filed involved Indonesian intellectual property laws and led to a change in the relevant provisions. More recently, the Community developed an explicit policy of reciprocity for financial services, clearly designed to extract concessions from Japan and the newly industrializing countries in the context of the GATT negotiations.[56]

The U.S. trade policy agenda expanded once again in the early 1990s. The cause was again political and centered on the NAFTA debate during the 1992 presidential campaign. To counter opposition within his party and from independent candidate Ross Perot, Clinton promised to "improve" on NAFTA by negotiating supplemental agreements on labor standards and the environment. This promise gave environmentalists an opportunity to enter trade politics and labor a chance to regain some of its declining voice on the issue. The exact status of these issues in Clinton's foreign economic policy became uncertain following the withdrawal of the request for fast-track renewal in late 1994. There is little question that they will be an integral part of American trade politics in the future, including discussion on regional agreements.

The Developing Countries in the GATT Regime

The growth of bilateralism is mirrored in changes in the position of the developing countries within the GATT system. Article XVIII of GATT, which covers infant industry protection and permits restrictions for balance of payments purposes, effectively allowed developing countries to pursue virtually any trade policy they pleased.[57] Following the last wave of decolonization and the emergence of a more politically aggressive third world bloc in the 1960s, the developing

55. See Jackson (1989, pp. 107–09). There are important differences between the new commercial policy instrument and 301. In particular, if a GATT dispute settlement process is applicable, it must be invoked first and carried to conclusion before counteractions may be employed. But there are also similarities: the emphasis on export promotion, the opportunity to engage issues not covered by GATT, and procedures that facilitate the initiation of actions.

56. See Nicolaides (1990, p. 210).

57. OECD (1992, pp. 93–111).

countries made claims for special and differential (S&D) status. The creation of the United Nations Conference on Trade and Development (UNCTAD) in 1964, the introduction of Part IV of GATT dealing with the developing countries in 1965, and the GATT waiver for the Generalized System of Preferences (GSP) in 1971 were testaments to the triumph of S&D principles and the drift toward an explicitly two-tiered system.

As recently as 1979, these claims were codified in the framework agreement to the GATT Tokyo Round accords and the decision entitled "Differential and More Favourable Treatment, Reciprocity and Fuller Participation of Developing Countries." Initially advanced by Brazil, the framework provided a further legal basis for the exceptions implied in the GSP, called for differential and more favorable treatment in the context of the Tokyo Round codes, granted permission to form regional arrangements even when they did not conform with the (minimal) restraints contained in article XXIV, and called for particularly special treatment for the least developed countries. The new decision also restated explicitly what had already been admitted in Part IV (article XXXVI [8]): that the developing countries were effectively exempt from the expectation of reciprocity.[58]

No sooner was the ink on the framework agreement dry than it became apparent that the developed countries' expectations for the advanced developing countries' participation in GATT were running in the opposite direction: toward more full developing country participation. One of the major purposes of negotiating separate code agreements in the Tokyo Round negotiations was precisely to limit free riding, including by the major developing countries. Nothing in the codes prevented countries from extending the benefits of the codes on a most favored nation basis, but the United States quickly made clear that it did not intend to do so.

The Subsidies Code was the most important for the developing countries. The 1979 Trade Agreements Act, which implemented the Tokyo Round agreement, explicitly stated that the United States would not have to meet an injury test to impose countervailing duties against nonsignatories. Were this not enough, the United States further developed a "commitments policy" for developing country signa-

---

58. On the political evolution of the framework, see Winham (1986, pp. 141–46). For a critical evaluation, see Wolf (1987a, 1987b).

tories: developing countries signing the code would also have to enter into a separate bilateral "commitment" to the United States that would demonstrate discipline regarding the use of subsidies. India challenged the United States on the point in a well-known fasteners case in 1980, but though the case was referred to a panel, India ultimately settled on the basis of a redrafted bilateral commitment.[59]

As can be seen in table 2-6, the major developing country exporters of manufactures have become signatories to many—though by no means all—of the Tokyo Round codes. The interesting exception is the general unwillingness to accede to the Code on Government Procurement. Predictably, the participation of less developed countries has been minimal.

The debate over the framework agreement during the Tokyo Round also raised the contentious issue of which countries should be considered "developing" and for how long, an issue later discussed under the rubric of "graduation."[60] The most concrete manifestation of the graduation debate was with respect to the GSP, and the conditions under which countries would no longer be eligible for these privileges. In 1988 the EC took the step of graduating Korea from its GSP, and in 1989 the United States followed suit by graduating the four East Asian newly industrializing countries—Korea, Taiwan, Singapore, and Hong Kong.[61] However, the significance of the concept of graduation was much broader and implied changing expectations about the behavior of developing countries on a range of issues, from the use (and abuse) of article XVIII, which allows exceptions for balance of payments reasons, to the demand that reciprocal concessions be tabled in the context of GATT negotiations.

The changing position of the developing countries in the GATT system was not simply a function of the expectations and pressures of the North; the South was also beginning to splinter into competing groups. The pattern of accession to GATT is revealing of these changes.[62] Nine developing countries acceded to GATT in 1948 and 1949, including Brazil and Chile, India, Pakistan, and Sri Lanka, and

---

59. See Jackson (1989, pp. 260–61).

60. See Frank (1979); Koekkoek (1988).

61. At the time of graduation, they were responsible for nearly 60 percent of all U.S. imports under the Generalized System of Preferences. U.S. International Trade Commission (1988, pp. 4–41).

62. The following is calculated from GATT (1993, Annex II).

Table 2-6. *Developing Country Signatories to the Tokyo Round Agreements (status as of December 31, 1992)*

Region and country	Standards	Government procurement	Subsidies	Customs valuation	Import licensing	Anti-dumping
Asia						
Hong Kong	A	A	A	A	A	A
India	A		A	A	A	A
Indonesia	A					
Korea	A		A	A		A
Pakistan	A		A		A	A
Philippines	A		A		A	
Singapore	A	A			A	A
Latin America						
Argentina	S		S	A	S	S
Brazil	A		A	A		A
Chile	A		A		A	
Colombia			A			
Mexico	A			A	A	A
Uruguay			A			
Africa						
Botswana				A		
Rwanda	S					
North Africa and the Middle East						
Egypt	A		A		A	A
Cyprus	A					
Tunisia	A					
Turkey				R		

Source: U.S. International Trade Commission (1993, pp. 17–18, table 2-2).
Note: A, accepted; S, signed, acceptance pending; R, reservation, conditions, or declaration.

several small Caribbean countries. From 1950 through 1965 thirty-one developing countries joined, but most of these accessions came from newly independent African states for whom the symbolic significance of participation in international organizations overshadowed substantive commitments; indeed, they were for the most part relieved altogether from negotiating their admission.[63] From 1965

63. Under Article XXVI (5c) colonies that become independent can become contracting parties through sponsorship by the parent country. Jackson (1989, pp. 45–46.)

1958

through 1980, the height of third world solidarity, the pace slowed, and only twelve developing countries joined.

Since 1980, however, there has been another burst of accessions: twenty-five countries. These included a number of new mini-states but also important medium-income countries, including Thailand and Tunisia, whose absence from GATT participation had become increasingly anachronistic. The largest bloc of major new entrants came from Latin America: Colombia, Mexico, Venezuela, and in the early 1990s, Bolivia and most of Central America.

The splintering of the Southern bloc, organized in the UN as the Group of 77 (G-77), did not result in rigid or fixed factions; allegiances were likely to shift from issue to issue. For example, the developing countries were initially united in their opposition to the inclusion of intellectual property rights under GATT; this issue broke along traditional North-South lines. By contrast, the Cairns Group, the lobby of agricultural exporters, included both developing and developed countries from its inception. Despite these particulars, however, it is possible to discern a clear line between those developing countries that sought to maintain a third worldist stance and those that increasingly came to see advantages to working within the GATT system.[64]

The former group, labeled the G-10, was led by two large countries with long histories of import substitution and extensive state intervention (Brazil and India) and included other countries with socialist governments (Cuba, Yugoslavia, Nicaragua, Tanzania).[65] The concerns of the G-10 were substantive and tactical. The group argued that much Tokyo Round business was unfinished and that the developed countries paid inadequate attention to their concerns about issues such as safeguards, textiles, and agriculture. The G-10 demanded more liberalization in these areas—through the principles of "standstill" and "rollback"[66]—before conceding to a new round of talks. The coalition also opposed the inclusion of services and intellectual property in the new round, both on "traditional" S&D grounds

64. Kahler and Odell (1989).
65. The remaining members were Egypt and Peru.
66. Standstill required that countries not adopt any GATT-inconsistent measures, that they exercise GATT rights with restraint and in a GATT-consistent manner, and that they refrain from pursuing policies designed to enhance their bargaining position in the round. Rollback required the phasing out of GATT-inconsistent measures.

that developing countries should not be expected to reciprocate in such areas, and on the tactical grounds that inclusion of trade, services, and intellectual property under the GATT umbrella would lead to undesirable linkage. Concessions on the new issues would not only be the price for movement on the traditional trade interests of the LDCs, but any agreement would open the door to the legal use of trade instruments to force liberalization in regard to services and other new issues.[67]

The more moderate group of developing countries, which included prominently the trading states of East and Southeast Asia and several Latin American countries, had a common interest in the traditional trade liberalization (market access) negotiations, in textiles and apparel, in tightening the use of CVDs and ADs, in circumscribing the use of safeguards, and in strengthening the GATT machinery of dispute settlement. Support also came from several developing country agricultural exporters in the Cairns Group, which sought movement on tropical products, and even from some African countries.[68] In return, this moderate coalition was willing to consider an extension of GATT rules into services and at least some of the other new agenda and deep integration issues. These developing countries (labeled the G-20) forged a common front with the countries participating in the European Free Trade Agreement—an unusual North-South alliance—and played a major role in generating a negotiating text for the Punta del Este meeting of the GATT contracting parties in September 1986, a text jointly sponsored by Colombia and Switzerland.

Detailed studies of the political process during the "pre-negotiation" phase leading up to the Punta del Este Declaration that launched the Uruguay Round negotiations, have demonstrated the steady erosion of support for the rejectionist stance championed by India and Brazil, an erosion of support only barely disguised by the concession of conducting the trade and services negotiations under legally distinct auspices.[69] The reasons for the collapse of the rejectionist front are several, including big changes within the coalition itself. In 1990 Brazil adopted several important liberalizing reforms; with these reforms, a reevaluation of

67. For a thoughtful statement of India's position by the chief negotiator, see Randhawa (1987).
68. On Africa's interests, see Oyejide (1990).
69. See Winham (1989); Drake and Nicolaides (1992); Low (1993, chap. 10).

foreign economic policy became inevitable.[70] These changes in Brazil reflected a broader phenomenon: the interests of the developing countries had simply diverged. The export-oriented states calculated that the grand trade-off of participating in the round, which might be characterized as new issues for old, was worthwhile. One reason was that several developing countries came to recognize that they might be able to develop a comparative advantage in certain services. The services agenda was therefore not necessarily inimical to their economic interests if the coverage of services was broad and certain phase-in provisions were allowed.[71]

For the major developing countries, however, the growth of bilateralism was unquestionably a principal reason for participating actively in the new round. First, full participation in the multilateral framework promised some check on the increasingly discretionary policies of the United States and to a lesser extent the EC. The new GATT round promised to clarify and tighten discipline regarding CVDs, ADs, and safeguards and to strengthen the machinery for surveillance, dispute settlement, and enforcement. Developing countries increasingly recognized that they could therefore gain rather than lose "autonomy" by fuller participation.

Second, the United States and to a lesser extent the European countries were beginning to pursue trade-related investment measures (TRIPs), intellectual property, and service issues bilaterally. This raised the question of why developing countries should offer concessions in bilateral talks when they could possibly extract greater gains on other issues of interest in a multilateral setting.[72]

Finally, it was clear that the trend toward conditional most favored nation set in motion during the Tokyo Round was unlikely to be reversed. This was most evident in the service negotiations. The principles outlined in the General Agreements on Trade in Services (GATS) mirrored those in the GATT itself with regard to most favored nation; states were required to extend benefits uncondition-

70. As an Indian observer remarked, "The moment Brazil reformed its economy we were left out in the cold." Professor Bibk Debroy, Indian Institute of Foreign Trade, cited in Hamish McDonald, "The Late Convert," *Far Eastern Economic Review,* December 5, 1991, pp. 64–65.

71. The potential importance of services to developing countries was stressed by Bhagwati (1984).

72. It also raised the question of whether developing countries would receive "credit" for the reforms that they had made.

ally. However, signatories could request exemptions from the application of MFN treatment for certain sectors or measures. These exemptions would in principle be phased out but were clearly used during the negotiations to secure concessions, especially from developing countries. The United States sought several exemptions, including in the "big" sectors of telecommunications and finance. The Europeans complained that such exemptions could undermine an overall agreement, but they did exactly the same thing for financial services. In October 1992 the EC informed thirteen countries—mostly advanced developing countries—that the EC's offers in financial services would be withdrawn if improvements in the EC's offers were not forthcoming.[73]

Such manipulation of the most favored nation principle occurred in addition to the tactical linkage across issues that one would expect in any multi-issue trade negotiation. All of the advanced developing countries were expected to table proposals that covered the issues on the GATT agenda.

Conclusion

Many external constraints operated on the developing countries in the 1980s and 1990s. Economic shocks, an expanding conditionality norm, growing bilateralism, and changes in the multilateral system pressed the developing countries toward greater integration with the world economy. Though many of these pressures centered on the shallow integration agenda of liberalizing trade and investment, they often spilled over into questions of deep integration.

This focus on international constraints is partly justified by the fact that the reformist trend among developing countries is worldwide. However, varied international pressures affect different developing countries in different ways. The coincidence of these international factors with domestic politics is also important to understanding the deeper integration of the developing countries; these matters are explored in chapters 3, 4, and 5.

73. U.S. International Trade Commission (1993, p. 21).

Chapter 3

East and Southeast Asia: Export-led Growth

THE major East and Southeast Asian developing countries—Korea, Taiwan, Hong Kong, Indonesia, Maylaysia, the Philippines, Singapore, and Thailand—have been highly integrated into the international trading system and thus are of great political interest to the advanced industrial states. The East Asian newly industrializing countries (NICs) not only dominate the exports of manufactures of the less developed countries, but that dominance has grown, as has the export share of the Southeast Asian countries. These countries are also experiencing very high growth rates of overall trade and deepening involvement in the world economy. The United States has been the major market for most of the eight, as it has for LDC imports more generally. The U.S. share of exports from Korea, Taiwan, and Hong Kong has fallen, partly reflecting their increasing concentration on Asia. However, U.S. imports from those countries surged when they failed to make adequate exchange rate adjustments to the falling dollar after 1985. In the mid-1980s, Taiwan and Korea ran very large current account surpluses. Moreover, the United States has continued to be an important export market for the booming trade of the new Southeast Asian NICs. Thus to the extent that there were adjustment problems associated with North-South trade in the 1980s, these problems were concentrated in the United States.

Because of the significance of these countries as exporters of manufactures, their increasing openness to trade, and their depen-

---

1. For a discussion of exchange rate policies in the four NICs, see Balassa and Williamson (1990).

Table 3-1. *Ten Largest Developing Country Exporters of Manufactures, 1980, 1990*

Country	Percent of total exports of developing countries	
	1980	1990
Hong Kong	17.1	19.8
Taiwan	16.6	16.2
Korea	14.9	15.8
Singapore	7.9	9.8
Brazil	7.1	4.2
Malaysia	2.3	4.2
Thailand	1.5	3.8
India	4.2	3.3
Mexico	1.2	3.1
Indonesia	0.5	2.4
East Asian NICs[a]	56.5	61.6
Southeast Asian NICs[b]	4.3	10.4
Total	73.3	82.6

Source: UN Conference on Trade and Development (1993, p. 17).

a. Includes Korea, Taiwan, Hong Kong, and Singapore.

b. Includes Malaysia, Thailand, and Indonesia.

dence on the American market—one would expect them to be vulnerable to external political pressure from the United States. This is particularly true of Korea, Taiwan, Hong Kong, and Singapore (tables 3-1, 3-2, 3-3). But the political pressure on the East Asian NICs did not simply stem from their export success; it was related to perceptions about the policy regimes that fostered that success. Hong Kong has long been an open, entrepôt economy, with virtually no restrictions on trade and investment. By contrast, governments in Singapore, Korea, and Taiwan have intervened extensively in their economies in various ways.[2] Korea and Taiwan pursued industrial strategies that included protection, subsidies to exporters, sectorally targeted industrial policies, and controls on the entry and behavior of foreign firms, especially in the service sector. Standards for the protection of intellectual property have been notoriously lax in East and Southeast Asia, and purposely so; copying of Western and Japanese technology has been an integral aspect of their strategy of industrial catch-up.

2. For different perspectives on the growth strategies of the NICs that emphasize the role of government intervention, see Amsden (1989); Haggard (1990); Wade (1990).

Table 3-2. *Export Growth in East and Southeast Asia (average annual growth rates)*
Percent

Nation and region	1950–60	1960–70	1970–80	1980–90	1990–91	1950–91
Korea	1.4	39.6	37.2	15.1	10.6	27.7
Taiwan	6.5	23.2	28.6	14.8	13.3	21.1
Hong Kong	−0.4	14.5	22.4	16.8	20.0	15.1
Indonesia	−1.1	1.7	35.9	−1.3	13.5	11.5
Malaysia	0.6	4.3	24.2	8.6	16.8	10.3
Philippines	4.5	7.5	17.5	3.8	8.0	9.2
Singapore	−0.1	3.3	28.2	9.9	12.0	11.7
Thailand	1.5	5.9	24.7	14.0	23.1	12.2
						+
Developing countries	3.1	7.2	25.9	2.2	5.8	11.1
Western Hemisphere	2.4	5.0	20.8	0.9	−0.3	8.7
Africa	3.9	9.2	21.7	−3.4	−1.2	9.4
Asia	3.1	7.7	30.1	3.5	9.5	12.8

Source: UN Conference on Trade and Development (1992, pp. 16–25).

A combination of rapid growth and an interventionist policy style has driven the international politics of deep integration in the East Asian NICs, as it did with Japan before them. During the past two decades, the United States has undertaken a string of bilateral actions against Korea and Taiwan, and to a lesser extent Singapore. These bilateral actions have gone through an evolution that reflects closely the changes in U.S. trade policy outlined earlier: use of voluntary export restraints (VERs) and orderly marketing arrangements (OMAs) for outright protectionist purposes beginning as early as the 1960s in textiles, a steady increase in unfair trade actions throughout the period, and an expansion of market-opening demands in the 1980s.

These demands first centered on the shallow integration issue of trade liberalization but later expanded to include elements of the deep integration agenda. Moreover, an increasingly dense network of bilateral consultations and governance structures has developed between the United States and Korea and Taiwan to oversee this process of deeper integration.

The emphasis on promoting manufactured exports is more recent in Thailand, Malaysia, and Indonesia, but it has been coupled with a number of deep integration reforms. American pressure has influenced this process, but so have other forces, including economic

Table 3-3. *Dependence of Asian Exporters on the U.S. Market*
Percent

| Country | Exports to U.S. market as a share of total exports | | | |
	1970	1980	1990	1992
Hong Kong	35.7	26.1	24.1	23.1
Korea	47.3	26.4	29.9	24.3
Indonesia	13.0	20.4	13.1	13.7
Malaysia	13.0	16.3	16.9	18.7
Philippines	41.6	27.7	38.0	40.0
Singapore	11.1	12.5	21.3	21.2
Taiwan	38.1	34.1	32.4	28.9
Thailand	13.4	12.4	22.7	22.5

Source: IMF, *Direction of Trade Statistics Yearbook;* Council for Economic Planning and Development (1993).

shocks and conditional assistance from donors and the multilateral institutions.

These external pressures on economic policy in the East and Southeast Asian countries have coincided with domestic economic and political circumstances that are at least relatively favorable to deeper integration. Most of the countries in the region initiated policy changes—typically under the leadership of strong or even authoritarian governments—that had already moved their economies in a more outward-oriented, if not liberal, direction. As a result, strong political forces, especially in the export-oriented private sector, are favorably disposed toward greater integration with the world economy and vulnerable to any threat of trade sanctions. External pressures for reform have taken place against the backdrop of robust economic growth, which makes it easier to accommodate potential losers. Even though there are ongoing controversies over policy measures, gradual and incremental liberalization and a willingness to realign policies around international norms have occurred. This is even true where democratization and political liberalization have taken place, as in Korea, Taiwan, the Philippines, and Thailand.

Outward-oriented development strategies and strong bilateral pressure from the United States have led the developing countries of the region to strongly support multilateralism. The general direction of policy among these countries also guarantees that regional cooperation initiatives are likely to take an open form, meaning that they will be liberalizing, nondiscriminatory, and inclusive. Developments in both APEC (Asia-Pacific Economic Cooperation) and the Association of Southeast Asian Nations (ASEAN), the two most important international cooperation efforts in the region, generally confirm these expectations. Until recently, however, there has been only a limited demand in the region for these associations to address the deep integration agenda or even to expand their institutional role significantly and that pressure came mainly from the United States. Consequently, American bilateralism remains an important political force for deep integration in the region.

The East Asian NICs

In comparison with many other developing countries, Korea and Taiwan have fairly liberal trade policies. Nonetheless, an early phase of liberalization in the 1960s initiated by strong, authoritarian governments stalled or was even reversed in the 1970s. Both countries settled into a bifurcated trade regime that coupled low barriers or duty-free entry for inputs to export industries with high, and often prohibitive, protection on a range of final products and targeted infant industries. Korea pursued an aggressive strategy of industrial deepening in the 1970s by emphasizing the development of heavy and chemical industries and a substantial concentration of the industrial sector.[3]

In the 1980s, the governments of Korea and Taiwan initiated import liberalization programs. There can be little doubt that American pressure affected the pace and composition of these efforts. In Taiwan, a major initiative announced in mid-1986 sought to reduce import tariffs and restrictions but also to improve the trade balance with the United States by granting preferential tariff treatment to trading partners based on the extent of bilateral imbalances. Following consultations with the United States in 1987, and in an effort to avoid Super 301 action, the government initiated two further large tariff cuts in 1988. In February 1989 a trade action plan sought not only to further liberalize trade but to boost consumption and investment in order to realize specific current account targets. Earlier 301 actions against Taiwan on customs evaluation forced the country to abide by the terms of the GATT Customs Evaluation Code and opened the market for U.S. beer, wine, and tobacco.

3. See Westphal (1990).

The Korean system has been far more protectionist, reflecting a more interventionist policy style and a political structure that allowed for much closer and more institutionalized business-government relations.[4] Besides tariffs, Korea has only gradually dismantled its import licensing system. Various special measures and high ministerial discretion in the conduct of trade policy blunted liberalization efforts. For example, a "surveillance system" allowed industry representatives to exercise a veto over imports if they posed competitive threats. Several industry-specific "special laws" overrode trade policy and gave ministries and allied industries vetoes over the import of certain products through the invocation of standards designed in a discriminatory way. As recently as 1990, a government-orchestrated austerity (anti-import) campaign resulted in the removal of foreign products from shelves, limits on promotional activities by foreign manufacturers, and even tax audits of owners of foreign cars.

Nonetheless, external pressure did contribute to import liberalization during the 1980s and 1990s. In 1984 the government launched the first of two back-to-back five-year tariff reduction programs.[5] The United States intensified its pressure on Korea after the presidential elections in 1988. As in Taiwan, the United States also used 301 actions to force the opening of markets for agricultural products, particularly beef, cigarettes, and wine. Bilateral consultations resulted in an agreement in October 1989 to lift all remaining quantitative restrictions or justify them under GATT rules by July 1997. The administration of Kim Young-Sam has continued the trend toward liberalization, including not only the lifting of formal barriers but the removal of informal import barriers that may have impeded market access. A five-year plan for tariff reduction was completed in January 1994, which brought the average tariff rate from 12.7 percent to 7.9 percent; more than 90 percent of Korean tariffs are now bound. The average tariff rate is now 6.2 percent for manufactured products, and most remaining disputes about formal barriers are likely to center on agriculture, where the government faces the stiffest resistance to continued opening.

American trade policy actions were by no means limited to shallow integration measures; bilateral talks encompassed the entire array of new items for discussion being negotiated in GATT, as well as issues

4. For a detailed account of the import regime, see Luedde-Neurath (1986).
5. On the liberalization programs, see Choi (1993, p. 94, table 1; p. 96, table 2); U.S. Trade Representative (1994, pp. 185–86).

on which no agreed international law exists. Three clusters of issues have been central to the U.S. strategy for opening markets in the East Asian NICs, and in the developing countries more generally: investment questions, services, and intellectual property. Though the United States by no means achieved all that it sought in these three areas, these issues illustrate how American pressures, and the underlying economic circumstances that gave rise to those pressures, set the agenda for several important policy reforms and resulted in bilateral arrangements that sometimes favored the United States over other investors.

Extensive use of export requirements and domestic content legislation and a lack of transparency in the entry process have characterized the investment rules in Korea and Taiwan. These policy measures were designed to limit competition to protect the domestic private sector. The course of Taiwan's policy is illustrative, though it is in general much more liberal than Korea's. Following consultations with the United States, Taiwan announced in 1987 that many sectoral restrictions on foreign direct investment would be lifted during 1988, though a long list of exceptions remained.[6] Trade-related investment measures were also an issue in Taiwan. Export requirements ranging from 5 percent to 50 percent were applied to some investments, and local content requirements remained a component of industrial policy. Following repeated U.S. complaints, Taiwan did eliminate export performance requirements and local content restrictions on these sectors. But in March 1986, the United States initiated a 307 investigation after Taiwan granted Toyota permission to build an auto plant subject to steadily rising export requirements. The United States protested the plan, and Taiwan agreed to eliminate performance requirements.

Negotiations in both countries covered virtually the entire array of services. Financial service negotiations in Korea, for example, show the difficulty of clearly separating the shallow integration objective of removing barriers and deep integration negotiations over the regulatory regime. As early as 1985, the United States

---

6. See U.S. International Trade Commission (1989, p. 122). Among those restricted sectors were agriculture, some services, and a number of industrial products being targeted for specific support. In June 1991 Korea revised its Foreign Capital Control Act to a negative list system, under which all investments not explicitly prohibited would be permitted. As in Taiwan, various restricted sectors remained.

launched section 301 actions on insurance. The result was the inclusion of two American insurers in what amounted to a government-supervised cartel, a prime example of how "liberalizing" measures may be undertaken in a fashion that is both discriminatory and maintains the existing system of controls intact.[7] U.S. negotiators gained a new instrument under the 1988 trade bill: the Treasury Department was authorized to determine whether countries manipulated exchange rates and to enter into talks with those countries on financial sector reform.[8] The legislation was clearly aimed at Japan and the East Asian NICs. The Treasury Department found that Korea was manipulating its exchange rate, and in February 1990, financial policy talks were launched. The talks established a new bilateral forum that would deal not only with macroeconomic and exchange rate issues but with the deregulation of the financial markets as well.[9]

After 1988, Korea balanced concessions to the United States with efforts to limit the competitive pressure on domestic financial firms. For example, in March 1990, immediately following the first talks on the financial sector, the government introduced a more flexible exchange rate system and addressed some of the problems facing foreign banks. Direct purchase of Korean securities was open to foreigners in January 1992, but the government limited foreign ownership of the total shares of a single company to 10 percent, and ownership by a single firm to 3 percent.[10] At the March 1992 talks on financial policy, the Ministry of Finance presented a document outlining a new blueprint for the comprehensive liberalization of the financial sector. But the plan maintained substantial discretion for the government by stipulating that future stages of liberalization would be contingent on the

7. See Cho (1987).

8. In 1989 Korea was also named as a priority country under section 1374(a) of the 1988 Trade Act, which allowed the United States to open bilateral negotiations on telecommunications. As with financial services, these were not merely shallow integration issues of import liberalization but included negotiations on the regulatory structure as well. U.S. International Trade Commission (1992, p. 123).

9. Virtually identical complaints can be heard about Taiwan. Even though it was not formally designated an "exchange rate manipulator," negotiations over services had begun in August 1985, when the United States submitted proposals for the liberalization of barriers to U.S. banking, insurance, shipping, and motion-picture distributing and leasing.

10. Given that some of the largest firms had been allowed to issue convertible bonds, these limits were quickly reached. *Business Korea*, February 1992, p. 27.

balance of payments, lower inflation, and a narrowing of domestic and international interest rate differentials.

Similar efforts at balancing foreign and domestic pressures are visible in the controversy over opening the domestic securities sector to foreign entry and resulted in discriminatory arrangements that paralleled earlier "liberalization" in insurance. In December 1990 Korea announced the criteria for those foreign securities firms that would be allowed to enter the domestic market. Among the considerations was the extent to which the entering firm contributed to the development of Korea's domestic industry, implying that joint ventures would be favored over wholly owned ventures. Moreover, the capital requirements were so high, and the scope of allowed business so vague, that many foreign firms refused to apply.[11] When the government announced the final list of firms granted entry, all of Japan's applicants were excluded on the ground that Korean entry into the Tokyo market was closed. Yet the interpretation given by financial analysts was that Korean firms were fearful of the cash-rich Japanese companies and that the list had been tailored to respond to American and British trade pressures.[12] In 1993 Korea's Kim Young-Sam administration launched yet another effort to liberalize foreign direct investment that included a strong emphasis on the service sector, a tacit recognition that previous efforts had been only partly successful.

The negotiations over the opening of the financial sector in both countries seem to constitute straightforward examples of how weak sectors were capable of resisting foreign pressure. But the government's preferences were not wholeheartedly for liberalization, either.[13] Korea feared that a full liberalization and deregulation of the financial system would reduce its ability to conduct industrial policy, which continued to rely on financial incentives and controls on bank portfolios even after the privatization had occurred. Taiwan's resistance to financial liberalization reflected a long-standing bias against the growth of private power; only with the gradual political liberalization of the late 1980s, and increased opportunities for the private

11. "Will Getting a Foot in the Door Pay-Off?" *Business Korea*, vol. 8 (January 1991), pp. 28–29.

12. "Bowing to U.S. and U.K. Trade Pressures," *Business Korea*, vol. 8 (April 1991), pp. 49–50.

13. On the political economy of financial market reform in the two countries, see Choi (1993); Cheng (1993).

sector to lobby for entry, did the government begin to liberalize the financial system.

Intellectual property raises somewhat different questions than do investment laws and service liberalization, since intellectual property issues demand not only legal changes but ongoing enforcement, compliance, and monitoring. Again, 301 action has been important in forcing policy change. In Korea, a comprehensive agreement was reached in 1986 following extremely acrimonious negotiations, and a new legal framework for intellectual property protection was put in place in 1987 based on amendments to national patent, copyright and trademark laws. The Office of the U.S. Trade Representative placed Korea on its priority watch list in 1992 for the second time. During 1991 and 1992, the Korean government passed a series of laws governing the enforcement of intellectual property rights and began revision of the patent law to improve the protection of computer chip designs as stipulated by the Uruguay Round agreement. Bilateral negotiations with Taiwan resulted similarly in changes in copyright, patent, and trademark protection laws between 1979 and 1985, and a comprehensive agreement in 1989.

In general, Korea and Taiwan have been willing to make concessions to the United States on the deep integration agenda. This stance is not simply a function of outside pressure; it also reflects the growing openness of their economies, the resulting sensitivity to external sanctions, and the gradual growth of internationalist forces in the private sector with an interest in closer integration. However, intellectual property also exemplifies some of the difficulties associated with deep integration under pressure. In some policy areas, there are high costs of monitoring and enforcement coupled with strong incentives to defect from agreements. Korea and Taiwan have responded to these problems by establishing new institutional units to oversee enforcement. Nonetheless, American firms have complained about lax enforcement, delays in bringing suit, and low penalties. As a result, threats, such as being placed on the Special 301 priority watch list, have been used to monitor compliance.

Second, complex regulatory issues, such as intellectual property and entry in the service sector, can be manipulated with discriminatory effect, giving rise to quasi-preferential agreements. The European Community's suspension of the Generalized System of Preferences (GSP) for Korea in 1988 was a direct response to lobbying by the powerful European Association of Chemical Manufacturers, which had become irritated at the Korean government's failure to grant European countries intellectual property protection similar to that extended to the United States under a 1986 bilateral agreement.

The ASEAN Exporters

The mix of factors affecting the course of economic policy in the major ASEAN exporters differs somewhat from the dynamics affecting the two larger East Asian NICs.[14] U.S. policy interest in Korea and Taiwan increased following the emergence of large current account surpluses in the mid-1980s. American policy interest in the major Southeast Asian countries also expanded with their increasing participation in world trade. However, the large ASEAN countries also experienced balance of payments difficulties in the 1980s, difficulties that shifted the balance of power within governments and acted as a spur to unilateral reform efforts. Balance of payments problems also increased the presence of the multilateral financial institutions in Thailand, Indonesia, and the Philippines, where these institutions played an active role in advancing and supporting reform efforts.

Although crises were by no means as severe as in the Latin American countries, they did give urgency to attracting foreign investment. These efforts gained importance in the 1990s as Japanese foreign direct investment slowed, and China became a more attractive site for foreign investors. Policy changes included both a relaxation of restrictions on foreign entry and expansion of incentives to certain activities, particularly export-oriented ones.

Indonesia offers a good example of a developing nation whose unilateral policy changes are triggered by balance of payments difficulties, in this instance associated with falling oil prices.[15] Indonesia's problems began in the early 1980s, and its initial response was to deepen the range and nature of trade and investment controls. Since 1985, however, the balance between the technocrats, who favored a more liberal policy stance, and the engineers, who supported an aggressive industrial policy, began to shift toward the technocrats. A

---

14. For an analysis that highlights these differences, emphasizing the less extensive nature of state intervention in Southeast Asia, see MacIntyre (1994).

15. Bresnan (1993, pp. 246–48, 251–52).

reform package announced in May 1986 made great steps toward granting foreign firms national treatment.[16] Demands for joint venture participation were relaxed, and new activities opened to foreign investors. In October, a stabilization plan supported by the donor consortium and the multilateral institutions included further liberalization of foreign direct investment, trade reforms, and partial deregulation of the transport and financial sectors.

In October 1988, yet another major package of trade liberalization measures ensued, as well as a comprehensive deregulation and liberalization of the financial sector. The purely domestic financial reforms are beyond the scope of this book, but two significant features of the reforms were the reduction of restrictions on the entry and operations of joint-venture banks and efforts in 1991 to increase capital adequacy requirements to meet international standards.

Malaysian trade policy has historically been relatively liberal by the standards of developing countries, but investment restrictions have been extensive in a political effort to favor indigenous Malay (*bumiputra*) firms.[17] In 1986, following a two-year slump in commodity prices, recession, and the emergence of balance of payments problems, Malaysia introduced new amendments to its foreign direct investment laws that included new tax incentives to foreign investors and greater flexibility on ownership and control. These revisions marked a sharp retreat from the pro-*bumiputra* policy. By exempting foreign firms from joint venture requirements, the Malaysian government even favored foreign firms over local Chinese ones. Further changes came in 1988, when it was admitted that the state-led heavy-industry push of the 1980s had been a mistake. Privatization emerged as a serious objective, creating further opportunities for foreign firms.

In Thailand, economic performance was consistent through the decade, and arguably for this reason, the reform process was more incremental.[18] Balance of payments difficulties early in the decade resulted in several politically difficult exchange rate adjustments and a series of structural adjustment loans from the World Bank. Objectives for trade policy were not fully realized, in part because the gradual opening of the political system provided new opportunities

16. Foreign firms were granted access to loans from the state-owned banks and the right to distribute through Indonesian intermediaries.

17. See Bowie (1994); Naya and others (1989, p. 123).

18. See Doner and Laothamatas (1994).

for private sector groups to maintain and secure advantages. By the end of the 1980s, however, the government interpreted restrictions on foreign equity participation flexibly to allow for 100 percent foreign ownership in some cases, especially in export industries.

The reform thrust has been much more limited in the Philippines, underlining the importance of domestic politics. The country experienced a profound debt crisis in 1983–84, which forced a difficult stabilization program and dramatically expanded the role of both IMF and World Bank conditionality. The fall of Marcos in 1986 allowed the Aquino government to undertake some reform measures under more favorable economic circumstances. Foreign sympathy for the new regime was substantial, and aid flows increased sharply. The government resumed a trade reform that had been suspended during the crisis by lifting many quantitative restrictions, and a new investment law marked a marginal liberalization over previous statutes.

However, the ability of the government to effect a more fundamental transformation of trade and investment policy was blocked by a strong coalition of nationalist political and economic forces, and a more open and politicized policymaking process after the transition to democracy in 1986. The 1987 investment law maintained numerous restrictions, and the effort by the government to complete an ambitious trade policy reform package died in the late days of the Aquino administration, leaving a number of unfinished shallow integration issues in the hands of the new Ramos government.

Economic policy reform in the ASEAN countries was not simply the result of economic crisis; bilateral relations with the United States and Japan also played an important role. However, as Peter Cowhey has argued, the bilateral strategies of Japan and the United States in the region are quite different.[19] Japan has worked primarily to achieve advantages for its firms; Japan's style of deep integration is an extension of the close business-government relations that characterize the Japanese economy. For the United States, by contrast, deeper integration takes the form of pressing countries to abide by universalistic rules.

The lure of attracting Japanese foreign direct investment was coincident with a dramatic increase in Japan's aid budget. Both events contributed to making Japan a much more significant political player

19. See Cowhey (1994).

in the region than it had been in the past. New studies on the Southeast Asian countries show that Japanese aid helped support programs initiated under the auspices of the multilateral institutions in both Indonesia and the Philippines.[20] But Japan's aid policy was probably most important on investment questions, and in this area, general rules proved less important than the ability of the Japanese government to provide support for its companies.

The most controversial Japanese program was a proposal by the Ministry of International Trade and Industry (MITI) for a New Asian Industries Development Plan. Conceived as an adjunct to Japanese industrial policy following the rise of the yen, the plan foresaw a new regional division of labor that would entail less raw materials processing in Japan, Japanese finishing of low-value-added products exported from Asian countries, and an expansion of joint ventures to facilitate domestic adjustment, especially among the small- and medium-sized businesses that were experiencing difficulties from the sharp appreciation of the yen.[21]

The plan was never officially adopted, but several of its main ideas have been carried out as part of other public and private initiatives. An ASEAN-Japan Development Fund, for example, has emphasized financing of infrastructure that would facilitate trade and investment. It was established in conjunction with Japan-ASEAN Investment Corporation, designed to steer Japanese investment toward worthy projects. Other quasi-public initiatives, such as the formation of the Japan International Development Organisation, Ltd. (JAIDO), were also undertaken. Formally established by the Keidanren, JAIDO is one-third funded by the Overseas Economic Cooperation Fund, the government's soft-loan agency.[22]

An important question is whether these public and private efforts have discriminatory effects. It could be argued that Japan's emphasis on liberalizing foreign investment and the provision of infrastructure constitute public goods that are to the benefit of all foreign investors, including non-Japanese firms. However, the rules governing foreign investment in the ASEAN countries, with the partial exception of Singapore, still involve substantial government discretion and negotiation, and thus private information can be critical in securing advan-

20. See Kingston (1993); Takahashi (1993).
21. Rix (1993b, pp. 28–29).
22. Lincoln (1992, p. 28).

tages or even entry. Infrastructure can also be designed to favor certain entrants. Richard Doner gives several examples of how government programs have the effect of creating industry- and even firm-specific advantages for Japanese multinationals.

> For example, members of the private sector do much of the groundwork for projects funded by the Japan-ASEAN Investment Corporation. Similarly, in Malaysia a JETRO- [Japan External Trade Organization] sponsored evaluation of press-die and precision-molding capacity made use of Japanese industry experts, and in Thailand, Japan International Cooperation Agency arranged for a visit by the founder of the Japanese mold-and-die association. . . . Further, many of these activities are industry-specific and result in a very impressive level of information. For example, JETRO and JICA officials are probably better informed than most officials in Thailand's Ministry of Industry on the competitiveness of various sectors of Thai industry.[23]

While Japanese policy focused great attention on the opportunities available to certain firms, American policy dealt with broader regulatory issues that affected American corporate interests. Bilateral pressures on the Southeast Asian countries have been somewhat less insistent and later in coming than was true in Korea and Taiwan, for the simple reason that the turn toward an export-oriented strategy in the region and the market opportunities for American firms resulting from extremely rapid growth have been more recent.

Investment and service issues have been in contention between the United States and some ASEAN countries, but the most highly visible conflicts have surrounded intellectual property protection.[24] Singapore and Thailand show interesting contrasts in the response of developing countries to somewhat similar external pressures. Singapore—which an industry-based alliance of firms with an interest in intellectual property dubbed the "world capital of piracy" in 1985—was the first ASEAN country to fall under external scrutiny in the early 1980s. British and American companies began to try to use local courts to deter pirating of music and software. When the U.S. government pressed the case in 1982, the Singapore government's response

---

23. Doner (1993, pp. 189–90).
24. The following paragraphs draw extensively on Uphoff (1990).

was that copyright protection was not, at that point, in the country's interest. Neither the provisions of the 1984 trade law nor the threat to curtail benefits from the Generalized System of Preferences was taken seriously, but pressure increased through domestic courts and through bilateral negotiations with the United States in 1985. The United States made clear the seriousness of its intention to manipulate GSP to achieve its objectives. External pressure made it difficult for the beneficiaries of the loose laws—effectively the pirating industry—to argue their case vigorously for fear of being the first to come under scrutiny. In 1987 a new copyright law passed: a bilateral agreement was signed that granted the United States most of what it wanted, and enforcement has generally been effective.[25] The reasons for this outcome were a strong and efficacious government that could control domestic resistance and enforce any agreement, a very high export orientation, and a policy interest in promoting higher technology sectors, for which intellectual property protection was particularly important.

Thailand presents a contrasting case. As in Singapore, U.S. pressure through GSP was the triggering event for reform. But when the cabinet announced its intention to change the laws, a political crisis ensued. Opponents—a loose coalition of students, labor leaders, academics, and the press—argued their case on both nationalist and economic development grounds. Rewriting Thai law to please the Americans was an unwarranted infringement of sovereignty and would be costly, especially for consumer of textbooks, pharmaceuticals, and computer software. The parliamentary debate quickly split on partisan lines, and the government was ultimately unable to pass a bill. The issue even played some role in the dissolution of the last Prem government. Prem's successor, the first elected civilian prime Minister in twelve years, was in an even more precarious political position and took a more nationalist stance than his predecessor. Talks with the United States broke off just before the deadline for negotiations on December 15, 1988, and the United States retaliated by withdrawing some GSP privileges. Efforts to respond to foreign pressure through enhanced enforcement stumbled on corruption and the sheer magnitude of piracy. In 1990 and 1991 the United States

25. A bizarre exception is a 1988 provision that allowed the copying of foreign copyrighted material that had been banned by the government for political reasons.

initiated two new 301 actions, one on copyrights, taken at the initiative of the U.S. Trade Representative, and a second on pharmaceuticals, initiated in response to industry complaints. The final resolution of these cases was blocked, however, by the political unrest in the country in 1992, and the United States finally decided that the problems would be addressed in the context of the GATT and ongoing bilateral negotiations. Thus even in the increasingly outward-oriented countries of the region, the political consensus on a number of deep integration questions is clearly absent, as is the capacity of the government to enforce domestic decisions even if they are reached.

Institutional Options for the Asian Developing Countries

The sources of resistance to deeper integration in East and Southeast Asia come not only from weak and uncompetitive sectors but also from reliance on various industrial policy practices that have succeeded in the past. These range from the use of the financial system to support favored sectors to self-conscious laxity in the enforcement of intellectual property rights.

Viewed over the long run, however, the region shows an unmistakable trend toward liberalization and deregulation, even if the pace of reform varies across countries. A major political issue is whether these trends in policy will create a demand for greater institutionalization and whether those institutions will address issues on the deep integration agenda.

Given their trade orientation, increasing openness, and political vulnerability, the East and Southeast Asian nations are among the developing countries with the greatest stake in the multilateral system. Korea and Singapore were active players in the Uruguay Round process. So were Malaysia and the Philippines, both of which are members of the Cairns Group of agricultural exporters. Thailand became a GATT member in 1982, and since 1979, Taiwan has effectively committed itself to play by GATT rules.[26] In 1990 Taiwan applied for GATT membership as a developed country, and in 1992 a GATT panel was formed to review the issues connected with Taiwan's accession.

26. See Liu (1990, p. 331).

However, a commitment to multilateralism is not incompatible with the development of regional arrangements. Controversies center on three issues:

—The geographic scope of possible regional arrangements, or the question of membership;

—The substantive issues any regional organization will consider, especially whether members will gravitate toward the deep integration agenda; and

—The extent to which regionalism will be accompanied by the development of formal organizations that might oversee deeper integration, including dispute settlement mechanisms.

Analyzing the politics of regional cooperation in East Asia remains somewhat speculative.[27] Initiatives such as Asia-Pacific Economic Cooperation (APEC) and the East Asia Economic Caucus are relatively recent. Others, including the Pacific Trade and Development Conference, the Pacific-Basin Economic Council, and the Pacific Economic Cooperation Council constitute networks of public and private actors but are not formal intergovernmental organizations and lack decisional authority.[28] A further complication arises because encompassing organizations that cover the entire region—however defined—will coexist with other subregional efforts, some of which might have implications for deeper regional integration. Table 3-4 summarizes membership in the major regional organizations.

The most firmly institutionalized of the subregional groupings is ASEAN. After years of unsuccessful attempts at a dirigist form of deep integration that attempted to allocate industrial activities among members, the organization announced its intention to create a free trade area at the fourth ASEAN summit in January 1992 in Singa-

27. Three useful collections that review regional developments from a political as well as economic perspective are Mack and Ravenhill (1994); Higgott, Leaver, and Ravenhill (1993); and Frankel and Kahler (1993).

28. The Pacific Trade and Development Conference series was initiated in 1968 with the support of the Japanese foreign ministry to consider various ideas for regional cooperation. Primarily academic, each conference has focused on a particular policy issue. Representatives of the private sector throughout the region formed the Pacific Basin Economic Council in the same year, which was also meant to provide a forum for the discussion of regional trade and investment questions. In 1980 a Pacific Economic Cooperation Conference was formed as a nongovernmental organization that included business executives and academics; government officials also attend, but in an unofficial capacity.

Table 3-4. *Main Regional Organizations in the Asian-Pacific Region*

Nation[a]	ASEAN 1967	PAFTAD 1968	PBEC 1968	PECC 1980	APEC 1989	AFTA 1992	EAEC 1993
Japan	O	●	●	●	●		□
South Korea	O	●	●	●	●		□
North Korea							b
Taiwan		●	●	●	●		□
China				●	●		□
Hong Kong			●	●	●		□
United States	O	●	●	●	●		
Canada	O	●	●	●	●		
Mexico			●	●			
Peru			●	●			
Chile			●	●			
Thailand	●	●		●	●	●	□
Indonesia	●	●		●	●	●	□
Philippines	●	●	●	●	●	●	□
Malaysia	●	●	●	●	●	●	□
Brunei	●	●		●	●	●	□
Singapore	●	●		●	●	●	□
Vietnam							□
Laos							□
Cambodia							□
Myanmar							□
Australia	O	●	●	●	●		
New Zealand	O	●	●	●	●		
Pacific Is.							
Russia				⊙			
EC	O			⊙			

Source: Ichimura (1994, p. 106).

a. ●, Members; O, Attend ASEAN Post-Ministerial Conference; ⊙, Observers; □, Expected initial members. ASEAN, Association of Southeast Asian Nations; PAFTAD, Pacific Trade and Development Conference; PBEC, Pacific Basin Economic Council; PECC, Pacific Economic Cooperation Council; APEC, Asia-Pacific Economic Cooperation; AFTA, ASEAN Free Trade Area; EAEC, East Asian Economic Caucus.

b. Unknown.

pore.[29] In January 1993 the common effective preferential tariff (CEPT) agreement was concluded. Its objectives were to reduce the tariff rates within ASEAN to 20 percent in five to eight years and to 0 percent to 5 percent in the following seven years.

Despite the announcement of certain sectors that would be subject to an accelerated liberalization schedule, governments retain great discretion to invoke a safeguard norm if liberalized industries experience distress. More important, the timetable for liberalization under the CEPT agreement varies from one country to the next. Despite various mechanisms to limit the extent of excluded products, such as the agreement that all exclusions must be made at the highly disaggregated eight- or nine-digit level, the numbers of exclusions claimed by Indonesia and the Philippines were very high.[30] Under the so-called "six minus x" formula, those countries seeking to move faster are not only free to do so but are under no obligation to extend the preferences granted to one another to the remaining "x" members. However, it is doubtful that this in itself will create adequate pressure on the slow-moving countries to revise their liberalization schedules. As the wider ASEAN experience shows, unilateral liberalization efforts have tended to lead, rather than follow, regional agreements.

The agreement has the longer-term goal of moving toward deeper integration, but observers of the process clearly view it as a staged, and therefore highly gradual, one in which shallow integration comes first. An assessment by Pangestu, Soesastro, and Ahmad says, "Once integration to facilitate trade of goods begins, the liberalization of services and factors of production will be a natural outcome to encourage the process of integration. Another corollary is that differences in industrial standards, customs classifications, environmental policies, investment policies, labor movements, taxes, and other domestic policies that can limit intra-regional trade will also need to be harmonized and standardized."[31] Given the tentative nature of the move toward shallow integration, however, these ambitions for deeper integration must be treated with some skepticism.

29. See Imada and Naya (1992).

30. The Philippines excluded 25.9 percent of its tariff lines, Indonesia 19.2, Malaysia 13.6, Thailand 9.6, Brunei 5.5. Singapore claimed no exclusions. Calculated from Ichimura (1994, p. 115.)

31. Pangestu, Soesastro, and Ahmad (1992, p. 348).

Innovation is occurring in other subregions, but it is taking a different form. An inventory of subregional initiatives would include the Greater South China Economic Zone (Hong Kong, Macao, Guangdon, and Fujian provinces, and Taiwan); the Growth Triangle (Singapore, Batam Island in Indonesia, and Johor Province); a Baht Zone in the border areas of Thailand, Laos, and Cambodia; and possible cooperation in the Japan Sea, particularly around the Tumin River, which would include China, the two Koreas, Japan, and Russia.[32] These experiments have been facilitated by national rules easing foreign direct investment and by more localized inducements negotiated among the parties. In this sense they represent small-scale efforts at closer integration. However none except the Australia-New Zealand Closer Economic Trade Agreement have addressed the national policy issues at the core of the deep integration agenda, and that agreement binds two developed economies.

There have been two competing conceptions of how wider regional economic cooperation might evolve; they differ on the definition of the geographic scope of the region and on the likely policy implications. One scenario sees an Asian bloc emerging.[33] This Asian scenario implies a three-bloc world, with a Japan-centered region competing with Western Hemisphere and European blocs. Such a development might emerge for two reasons. First, trade frictions between East Asia on the one hand and the United States and Europe on the other could escalate to the point at which an inward-looking regionalism seemed to be a viable policy alternative for ASEAN, the NICs, and Japan. Second, an Asian bloc might emerge because intraregional trade and investment deepened so much that they provided an economic foundation for closer political and institutional cooperation.

It has been suggested that Japanese investment and aid could be the glue for an intra-Asian bloc linking Japan with the developing countries of the region. Initiatives such as the New Asian Industries Development Plan and the ASEAN-Japan Development Fund dis-

32. See Chia and Lee (1993).

33. There has been substantial analysis of the economics of integration in the region, but much of the speculation on the emergence of a coordinated yen bloc has been journalistic. See "Yen Bloc Survey," *Economist*, July 15, 1989, pp. 5–20. However, Doner (1993) and Lincoln (1993, pp. 160–200) provide serious analysis of the organizational—rather than economic—factors that might contribute to the emergence of a de facto bloc.

cussed earlier suggest a particular form of deep integration: regional planning efforts that weave together overseas development assistance, foreign investment, and export promotion.[34]

Yet there are two powerful reasons why the Asian scenario is unlikely to develop, at least not in a preferential way. First, the East and Southeast Asian countries continue to depend heavily on the United States as an export market, and there is little sign that Japan is capable of or willing to substitute for that role. The initial fear of a move toward a three-bloc world seems to have been linked with a temporary phenomenon: the spurt of growth in intraregional trade and investment associated with the strong yen in the late 1980s. Several recent studies have expressed doubt about the trend toward a relative deepening of economic regionalization.[35] Skepticism arises because Asia's interregional trade and investment are growing as fast as or faster than intraregional trade and investment. The political implications are obvious: export interests in the major developing countries have little incentive to design institutions that would exclude major trading partners, particularly the United States.

A second source of skepticism about an exclusive East Asian grouping concerns Japan. Japan's strong investment position in the region is a political liability rather than an asset, since it underscores the fact that Tokyo would dominate any exclusively Asian zone. For smaller countries, nondiscrimination in extraregional trade and investment constitutes a counterweight to Japanese influence.

Regional reactions to the Malaysian proposal for an East Asian Economic Grouping confirm these doubts about the likelihood of an Asian scenario. The proposal, advanced in the wake of the temporary collapse of the Uruguay Round talks in 1990, called for the creation of an economic bloc that would include ASEAN, Burma (Myanmar), Hong Kong, China, Taiwan, South Korea, and Japan. Australia, New Zealand, Canada, and the United States were explicitly excluded. Though the initial proposal was far from clear, it suggested the need to strengthen East Asia's bargaining power within GATT and to counter other regional groupings by moving toward an East Asian free trade area.

34. See Unger (1993); Lincoln (1992, 1993); Doner (1993), and (Rix 1993b).
35. See Petri (1993); Frankel and Kahler (1993); Fishlow and Haggard (1992); Anderson and Norheim (1993); Cowhey (1994).

Asia's reaction to the proposal was markedly cool. Japan, Korea, and Indonesia voiced reservations early. Singapore was willing to consider the proposal but emphasized three conditions: that the EAEG be consistent with GATT, that it be "parallel" to the interests of the Asia-Pacific Economic Cooperation initiative, which included Australia, New Zealand, and the United States, and had strong backing from all four; and that it not be viewed as a substitute for ASEAN.

The U.S. response was even more chilling. American ambassador to Japan Michael Armacost signaled that the grouping could "encourage economic rivalry" between Japan and the United States.[36] By early 1991 the Japanese were already quietly indicating their disapproval: one official was quoted as objecting that "[Japan does] not believe that the world should be sliced up like a watermelon into major economic blocs."[37] In October ASEAN formally dropped the idea in favor of a looser consultative body within APEC, the East Asian Economic Caucus.

If trade patterns do not seem to support the emergence of an Asian bloc, they do appear more propitious for the establishment of a Pan-Pacific organization that includes Asian countries and the United States, Canada, Australia, New Zealand, and other countries in the Western Hemisphere. Not only does the American market remain critical for Japan, the NICs, and ASEAN, but U.S. trade is increasingly concentrated in Asia too. Combined, the Western Hemisphere and Pacific Asia now account for more than 70 percent of Pacific Asian exports. Despite the attention given to the prominence of Japanese foreign direct investment in integrating Asia, American and Japanese investment have also been important in trans-Pacific trade.[38] If there is evidence of regional deepening, it points to the development of a larger Pacific bloc. Growth has been robust, the economies of the region are relatively open, and outward-oriented trade and investment regimes offer a common policy baseline for deeper integration.

As table 3-4 shows, several transnational organizations and forums with inclusive conceptions of membership have emerged in the region

36. See Hamish McDonald, "India under Siege," *Far Eastern Economic Review,* April 18, 1991, pp. 70–71.
37. Michael Vatikiotis and others, "Building Blocs," *Far Eastern Economic Review,* January 31, 1991, pp. 32–33.
38. Dennis Encarnation (1991) has documented this most clearly.

in the past two decades.[39] Most of these organizations have become a locus for the formation of transnational networks, but they have not graduated to the status of policymaking institutions, let alone emerged as a forum for consideration of the agenda for deep integration. The one intergovernmental institution that has the potential to take on this task is the Asia-Pacific Economic Cooperation (APEC) forum, initiated by Australia in 1988. Hong Kong, Taiwan, and China attended the 1991 meetings in Seoul, revealing some of the opportunities for wider cooperation that may emerge as a result of the end of the cold war. At the 1992 meetings, a small secretariat was authorized.

The 1993 meeting in Seattle, coming on the heels of President Clinton's victory in securing passage of NAFTA, gave another big boost to the organization and showed some incipient signs of movement toward a more operational form. The summit adopted a trade and investment framework and created a permanent committee on the topic to replace the Informal Group on Trade Liberalization; this alone marks an expansion of the organization's principal ambitions. Working groups on telecommunications, marine resources conservation, and fisheries also provide opportunities for deeper functional cooperation.

The 1994 APEC summit in Indonesia produced further institutional development, including agreement on a nonbinding investment code. The most dramatic outcome of the Jakarta summit, however, was the adoption of a proposal contained in the second report of the Eminent Persons Group to commit APEC members to free trade within the region by 2020, with the advanced industrial states obligating themselves to that goal by 2010. With the political success of the 1993 and 1994 summits, it became increasingly clear that APEC was the central forum around which further regionwide institutional development was most likely to occur.

Throughout APEC's evolution, its advocates have stressed the "open" nature of Pacific regionalism, meaning both a commitment to the principle of nondiscrimination and a willingness to consider new members.[40] Asian governments have strongly resisted the formation

39. By inclusive conceptions of the region, I mean those organizations that encompass North America, Australia, and New Zealand.

40. The 1992 declaration by the Pacific Economic Cooperation Council on "open regionalism" is a clear statement of the principle of nondiscriminatory regionalism. Cheit (1992). See also Yamazawa (1992).

of a formal free trade area that would discriminate against outsiders, in part because their trade dependence and increasingly diversified trade structures make it an economically questionable strategy.

Critics of open regionalism, particularly in the United States, have argued that commitment to nondiscrimination serves to dilute APEC's political clout and invites free-riding by nonmembers, particularly in Europe. In its weakest form, nondiscriminatory "open regionalism" would involve few firm commitments and leave all decisions to national governments about how far and fast they are willing to liberalize.

The compromise reached at the 1994 summit allowed countries to extend the benefits of APEC liberalization to nonmembers on an unconditional basis; indeed, the summit statement encouraged such unilateral liberalization. However, as Fred Bergsten has argued, the very size of the APEC economies leaves open the possibility that the outcome of the summit could be used to leverage global trade negotiations.[41]

Open regionalism also implies an open accession clause. China, Taiwan, and Hong Kong joined APEC in 1992, Mexico, Papua New Guinea, and Chile were added in 1993 and 1994, and attended the Bogar summit. Recently, the membership issue has been complicated by fears of congestion, and it was agreed before the 1993 summit to postpone the possibility of new members for three years. However, in the future APEC may easily encompass more members from the Western Hemisphere.

An interesting feature of APEC that differentiates it from free trade areas and customs unions elsewhere in the world is that it has moved toward negotiations on deep integration issues simultaneously with, and even prior to, agreement on shallow integration questions. The first report of the Eminent Persons Group (EPG) to the APEC ministers spelled out an ambitious agenda that included not only free trade in the Asia-Pacific region, but a regional investment code; cooperation on issues of deep integration, including competition policy, product standards, and testing and monitoring procedures; environmental protection; and the establishment of a procedure for settling APEC disputes.[42] The idea of creating a free trade area ran into great resistance at the Seattle summit and was effectively scuttled over the course of 1994. However the second report of the EPG,

41. See Bergsten (1994).
42. See APEC (1993); Elek (1992a, 1992b).

completed in July 1994, contained other deep integration proposals, including an investment code, discussion of harmonization of standards, environmental and competition policy, and the establishment of a dispute settlement mechanism.[43] The 1994 summit signaled that there was high-level support for these objectives.

Despite recent developments in APEC, institutions in the Pacific appear substantially weaker than those in Europe or the Western Hemisphere.[44] One reason is that despite the extremely rapid growth of trade and investment, there has not been strong demand within Asia for greater policy coordination. The region thus appears to disconfirm the theory that heightened interdependence creates the demand for deeper integration. The openness of the U.S. market, natural economic forces of proximity, and the complementarity of national policies have produced greater economic interdependence without extensive coordination at the regional level; for some of its proponents, this state of affairs is precisely what open regionalism means.[45]

Two other political reasons account for the limited and weakly institutionalized nature of regional integration in the Pacific. The first concerns the political and economic heterogeneity of the region. In the past, a broader Pacific organization faced vexing problems of membership. Some difficulties had to do with the legacy of the cold war, especially the problem of accommodating the People's Republic of China, Taiwan, and Hong Kong in one organization. Related problems center on ASEAN's fear that its integration effort would be diluted by inclusion in a wider organization, or that a larger organization would become a vehicle for the exercise of influence by Japan and the United States. This fear remains one of the most important barriers to deeper integration. However, the greatest difficulty related to membership is the prospect of diseconomies of scale. Not only do larger numbers make decisionmaking on the tasks of deep integration more difficult, but it implies that countries with widely divergent interests—from socialist China to Japan and the United States— would be drawn together.

Second, differences between the two major powers in the region create political problems. The United States wants to push for deeper

43. See APEC (1994).
44. For a succinct review, see Kahler (1993).
45. Cheit (1992); Drysdale and Garnaut (1993).

integration—or at least to press for that part of the deep integration agenda in America's interest—but Japan is cautious. One reason for this caution is the American penchant for universal rules compared with the ability of the Japanese to achieve their objectives without them.[46] An equally compelling reason for Japan's skepticism is the fear that calls for deeper integration will be little more than a weapon trained on Japan; several other Asian countries share this concern. To the extent that Japan is interested in deeper integration, it is likely to focus less energy on the development of universal rules and more on building mechanisms for dispute settlement that would restrain the United States from pursuing its deep integration agenda.

Even if APEC takes off, bilateral pressure from the United States will remain an important political force for deeper integration in the region. These bilateral relations are moving toward greater institutionalization. In the late 1980s, proposals were made for free trade agreements between various East Asian countries and the United States, and a number of them were analyzed in depth by the International Trade Commission, including plans for Japan, Korea and Taiwan.[47] Expert opinion generally rejected the idea of the possibility of reaching such agreements, and none has progressed.

Other forms of bilateralism have gained ground, not only with Japan but with the developing countries in the region. A visit by President Bush to Seoul in January 1992 gave rise to what was subsequently known as the "President's Economic Initiative," a comprehensive effort to negotiate various deep integration issues: standards, regulatory and customs procedures, and technology and investment laws. In 1992 similar steps were taken toward the negotiation of a framework agreement with Taiwan that would result in the establishment of a permanent Council on Trade and Investment. As with the new Korean initiative, the agenda touched on several deep integration issues, including services and intellectual property.[48]

One response to the growing importance of the ASEAN countries was discussion of the formation of some special relationship with the United States, as exists between the United States and Northeast Asian countries. Before 1977, no formal ties existed between the

46. This is the theme of Cowhey (1994).
47. See the essays on Japan, Korea, Taiwan, and ASEAN in Schott (1989).
48. See U.S. International Trade Commission (1993, pp. 72–74).

United States and ASEAN as an entity. The American defeat in Vietnam and the Vietnamese invasion of Cambodia increased ASEAN's interest in securing continued American involvement in the region. Moreover, the United States remained ASEAN's largest market, and the rise of the new protectionism also began to affect the "second-tier" NICs. ASEAN had developed a weak consultative arrangement with the EC beginning in 1972, but ASEAN's foreign economic policy did not take firm institutional shape until the initiation of a "dialogue" program with the EC and with the five developed countries of the region—Australia, Canada, Japan, New Zealand, and the United States—in 1977. Since 1979, these meetings have been institutionalized in postministerial conferences known as the six-plus-five meetings.

Not until 1988, however, was a new step taken toward further cooperation in the form of an ASEAN-U.S. initiative.[49] A joint research study conducted by Southeast Asian and American scholars proposed a broad umbrella agreement based on several principles, including free trade and capital movements, commitment to multilateralism, and "standstill and rollback" of trade barriers. This umbrella agreement would have established broad guidelines and an administrative and bargaining structure, including a consultative committee, for the negotiation of subsidiary agreements on subjects such as subsidies, double taxation, and safeguards. Included on the agenda were many deep integration issues, especially investment, services, and intellectual property. The consultative committee would also have studied the possibility for the negotiation of a U.S.-ASEAN free trade area. The idea of an overarching initiative stumbled on legal technicalities, but the United States signed a memorandum of understanding in December 1990 under which bilateral agreements could be reached, and such agreements were signed with the Philippines in 1989 and with Singapore in 1991. Under the Clinton administration, the United States proposed another regional initiative with ASEAN under the rubric of the U.S.-ASEAN Alliance for Mutual Growth. As with the agreements brokered with Korea and Taiwan, these initiatives will provide the United States instruments of pressure and surveillance as much as two-way exchange.

Are these regional and bilateral initiatives in the Pacific compatible with the multilateral order? On balance, developments in the region

49. Naya and others (1989).

confirm the view that multilateralism and open regionalism can co-exist while furthering the objective of deeper integration. There is little threat that Asian regionalism will evolve in a discriminatory direction.

The relationship between bilateralism and a rule-based multilateral system is more complicated. American efforts have focused on issues that the United States would like to bring under multilateral surveillance and rules. Bilateral actions on investment, services, and intellectual property ran parallel to U.S. policy toward the evolving GATT round. In some cases, however, both American and Japanese bilateral pressures were deflected through preferential and quasi-preferential agreements. Even when liberalization measures were not designed with the intention to discriminate—and in several important cases they clearly were—the United States, and to a lesser extent Japan and the EC, was able to set the policy agenda in ways that favored their firms over other entrants. Whether discriminatory or not, there is little reason to believe that such efforts at influence, long a feature of the foreign economic policy of the big countries toward the small ones, are likely to disappear.

Chapter 4

Latin America

T HE most striking difference between Latin America and East and
Southeast Asia during the 1980s was the depth of the economic
crises that swept across the Western Hemisphere (table 4-1). Though
several Asian countries experienced external shocks in the 1980s that
affected national policies, the economic difficulties in Latin America
were much more persistent and deep seated. The initial challenge
posed by these crises centered on balance of payments adjustment
and the stabilization of runaway inflation. However, both the crises
and initial adjustment efforts also raised the broader question of the
appropriateness of the underlying development strategies Latin American governments had pursued in the post-World War II period.

At the heart of this reassessment was the question of how the Latin
American countries would be integrated into the international economy. The region's rapidly declining share of global trade and investment constituted a powerful motive for shallow integration efforts.[1]
By the early 1990s all of the major Latin American countries had at
least attempted some trade reform. Balance of payments difficulties,
especially the evaporation of access to foreign borrowing, also put a
very high premium on attracting foreign capital. Consequently, the
traditional battery of restrictive barriers to foreign direct investment
fell.

The reform movement was by no means limited to these shallow
integration measures. Latin American governments also initiated
sweeping measures that ranged from privatization, to the deregulation

1. See Fishlow and Haggard (1992).

75

Table 4-1. *Macroeconomic Performance in Selected Latin American Countries, 1982–92*

Nation	Per capita GDP growth[a]		Inflation[b]	
	1982–86	1987–92	1982–86	1987–92
Argentina	−0.9	0.6	316.5	446.7
Bolivia	−5.0	0.7	776.5	15.8
Brazil	1.3	−1.3	157.9	850.8
Chile	−2.0	5.2	21.2	19.1
Colombia	0.8	2.0	20.6	27.3
Mexico	−2.6	1.0	73.2	48.4
Peru	−1.7	−4.9	102.7	733.1
Uruguay	−3.0	2.7	53.0	80.5
Venezuela	−2.3	1.6	10.2	40.2

Source: World Bank (1993a, p. 7, table 1.1).
a. Constant prices, percent change.
b. Growth in consumer price index, compound growth rates.

of certain markets, including financial markets, to the strengthening of protection for intellectual property. Some of these policy measures seem wholly domestic in origin and nature. In three important respects, however, they are germane to a discussion of deep integration. First, several reforms were designed to conform to existing or emerging international rules and reflected changing expectations about Latin America's participation in the multilateral system. The deregulation of financial services and the strengthening of intellectual property protection—both issues on the Uruguay Round agenda—are examples. Second, as in East Asia, bilateral pressures from the United States and the international financial institutions affected the reform movement. Finally, even when these pressures were absent, reforms represented unilateral emulation of the norms and practices of the advanced industrial states, generally undertaken with an eye to stabilizing the environment for foreign investors. Regulatory changes in securities and exchange laws and competition policy are examples.

Though economic crisis provides the broad context for these reform efforts, the timing of reform in various countries was influenced in important ways by domestic and international politics. The role of domestic political factors can be highlighted by underlining again the contrast to the East and Southeast Asian countries. In Korea and Taiwan, authoritarian governments launched outward-oriented reforms in the 1960s, well in advance of the transition to democratic politics. In Indonesia, Singapore, and Malaysia, authoritarian or dominant party governments have retained power, and in Thailand political liberalization was extremely gradual and even briefly reversed in 1991. In short, in all of the countries in the region except for the Philippines economic reform preceded political liberalization and democratization. Moreover, when democratization did occur, it usually took place in the context of robust economic growth. These political conditions were most often favorable to a gradual consideration of the agenda for deep integration.

These political conditions have been much less common in Latin America, where the coincidence of severe economic crisis and transitions to democratic rule have resulted in a significant politicization of economic policy. Three sequences of economic and political change can be distinguished.[2] In Chile and Mexico, strong governments undertook wide-ranging adjustments and sustained them before full transitions to democracy occurred. Not coincidentally, these governments were among the region's "early adjusters" and have moved the farthest in embracing the deep integration agenda. Venezuela and Colombia had consolidated democracies at the time crises hit, and both nations undertook adjustment measures within that context. Some success was achieved in Colombia, but violent and politically destabilizing reactions occurred in Venezuela.

Brazil, Argentina, Bolivia, and Peru exhibit a third pattern. These countries faced daunting economic adjustments at the same time that they were undergoing transitions to democratic rule; economic and political reform overlapped. New democratic governments in all four countries produced profound policy failures in the 1980s as a result of delays in adjusting or as a result of failed "heterodox" adjustment efforts. Radical reform efforts followed under the subsequent democratic governments of Color, Menem, Paz Estenssoro, and Fujimori, typically launched through controversial executive initiative. These reformist democratic governments exploited crises early in their terms to link stabilization efforts with broader economic policy changes that typically included both shallow and deep integration measures.

Latin America differs from East Asia not only in domestic politics, but also in the nature of the U.S. role in the region. The United States

---

2. A more detailed analysis along these lines is contained in Haggard and Kaufman (forthcoming).

did exert direct pressure on its major trading partners in the region, especially Mexico and Brazil; these pressures have been a factor in both shallow and deep integration reforms in both countries. However, U.S. policy toward Latin America differs from that toward East Asia in the existence of two regional integration initiatives: the Enterprise for the Americas Initiative (EAI) and the North American Free Trade Agreement (NAFTA).

Though launched separately, the two initiatives quickly became linked. The EAI held out the promise to negotiate bilateral free-trade, or at least framework, agreements. NAFTA—with its open accession clause—signaled the substantive form such agreements would take, in effect, the baseline against which future agreements would be measured. In combination, these initiatives forced governments to consider the Mexican example and to weigh the merits of the adjustments that would be required for possible accession.

Mexico, however, had already undertaken substantial reforms before the negotiation of NAFTA. An overview of the political economy of reform in the region suggests that this pattern is a general one: the explosion of integration schemes has followed, rather than led, national policy changes. This course of events does not diminish the political significance of NAFTA, however. On the one hand, Mexico's commitments under NAFTA have become a focal point for discussions of deep integration in Latin America. On the other hand, EAI and NAFTA have contributed to a countermovement of homegrown Latin American integration efforts based on an alternative, and "shallower," conception of the path that regional integration should take. The first step toward the reconciliation of these competing ideas was taken at the Miami summit in December 1994, which held out promise for the creation of a Western Hemisphere Free Trade Area.

Economic Reform in Latin America

No doubt the 1980s will be viewed as a turning point in Latin America's economic history. Governments jettisoned long-standing models of import substitution and extensive controls, regulation, and state intervention in favor of a package of reforms John Williamson has called "the Washington Consensus."[3] However, the timing of the reform movement in the region suggests the importance of domestic political factors as well as external shocks. One can see the significance of these elements by tracing the spread of economic reform in the region, beginning with shallow integration measures and moving toward the more recent consideration of deep integration.

Trade liberalization has been extensive and encompassed a lowering and rationalization of tariffs and the elimination of quantitative restrictions (table 4-2). The Southern Cone was the pioneer in trade liberalization, but not all of the initial experiments held.[4] The Southern Cone trade reforms were one component of a larger political project undertaken by highly coercive military regimes that was designed to dismantle the regulatory and protectionist policies of earlier decades. Between 1975 and 1979, the Pinochet government in Chile unilaterally eliminated quantitative restrictions and reduced tariffs to a uniform 10 percent rate. There was a brief reversion to a higher tariff level following the economic crisis of 1981–82, but by the mid-1980s tariffs had once again been lowered to their earlier uniform low rate. In Uruguay and Argentina, by contrast, governments reversed trade reform efforts in the face of crises produced by unsustainable exchange rate and fiscal policies and unregulated private-sector borrowing. Liberalization was put on hold for nearly a decade before being resumed under new democratic governments.

Bolivia and Mexico were the next to move; with Chile, they constitute the continent's "early adjusters."[5] Both initiated wide-ranging trade liberalization programs in 1985–86 in the wake of crises. Bolivia's reform was a radical one. The government established a two-tier structure with a maximum tariff rate of 10 percent and eliminated all licensing requirements except for sugar and wheat.[6] The background to this reform was the profound economic mismanagement of the first democratic government under President Hernán Siles Suazo

3. See Williamson (1990, p. 7). Williamson's list included reducing fiscal deficits, shifting expenditure priorities, tax reform, interest rate reform, exchange rate adjustment, trade liberalization, liberalization of rules governing foreign direct investment, privatization, deregulation, and protection of property rights.
4. See Papageorgiu, Michaely, and Choksi (1991).
5. See World Bank (1993a, p. 6).
6. See U.S. International Trade Commission (1992, p. 6–6).

Table 4-2. Trade Reform in Latin America

Country (prereform year, postreform year)	Average unweighted legal tariff rates (percent)[a]		Tariff range (percent)[a]		Coverage of quantitative restrictions (QRs) on imports (percent of tariff lines, unless otherwise noted)[b]		Openness of economy (imports + exports as percent of GDP, 1980 prices)	
	Prereform	Postreform	Prereform	Postreform	Prereform	Postreform	Prereform	Postreform
Argentina (1987, 1991)	42[P]	15	15–115[P]	5–22	62[c]	A few	38.57	54.32
Bolivia (1985, 1991)	12[M]	8	n.a.	5–10	n.a.	Minimal	57.51	83.97
Brazil (1987, 1992)	51	21	0–105	0–65	39	Minimal	21.17	25.27
Chile (1984, 1991)	35	11	35	11	Minimal	0	44.96	56.34
Colombia (1984, 1992)	61	12	0–220	5–20	99	1	28.23	32.66
Costa Rica (1985, 1992)	53[P]	15[P]	0–1400[P]	5–20	n.a.	0	58.66	78.97
Ecuador (1989, 1992)	37[P]	18	0–338[P]	2–25[d]	100	0	48.73	50.84
Guatemala (1985, 1992)	50[P]	15[P]	5–90	5–20	6[c,e]	0[e]	31.31	35.56
Honduras (1985, 1992)	41[P]	15[W,P]	5–90	5–20	n.a.	0[f]	62.82	61.76
Jamaica (1981, 1991)	n.a.	20	n.a.	0–45	n.a.	0[f]	105.51	163.49
Mexico (1985, 1990)	24[W]	13[W]	0–100	0–20	92[c]	20[l]	22.63	34.31
Paraguay (1988, 1991)	n.a.	16	n.a.	3–86	n.a.	A few	51.01	63.14
Peru (1988, 1992)	n.a.	17	0–120	5–25	100	0[g]	30.37	41.58
Trinidad and Tobago (1989, 1991)	n.a.	41[P]	n.a.	0–103[P]	n.a.	A few[h]	124.89	141.21
Uruguay (1987, 1992)	32	18	10–55	12–24	0	0	38.04	45.10
Venezuela (1989, 1991)	37	19	0–135	0–50	40	10[h]	49.25	53.29

Source: Alam and Rajapatirana (1993, p. 45).

n.a. Not available.

a. P: including tariff surcharges; M: import-weighted average tariff; W: production-weighted average tariff.

b. Even where tariff line coverage is small, domestic production coverage may be significant.

c. Of domestic product.

d. Ecuador also has a specific tariff of 40 percent on automobiles.

e. Guatemala has significant QRs for health and safety reasons; prereform, they covered 29 percent of domestic manufacturing production.

f. Some QRs do exist for health and safety reasons.

g. On agricultural products only.

h. Another 8 percent of tariff items are restricted because of health reasons; prereform, the number was 5 percent.

and the emergence of hyperinflation. Siles's technocratic team attempted to respond to the sharp decline in external finance with standard stabilization measures, but the cabinet and affected interest groups blocked the measures. Opponents included business and Siles's allies in the Bolivian labor movement. Facing rapidly accelerating inflation, the legislature granted Siles's successor, Victor Paz Estenssoro, extraordinary executive powers. On coming to office, he launched a comprehensive stabilization and structural adjustment initiative that included radical trade reform.

Mexico's program was a more gradual one, but crises also played a crucial role.[7] In its initial response to the debt crisis in 1982, the government held the view that stabilization should precede structural adjustment, and trade reform was therefore limited primarily to reversing the controls imposed at the height of the crisis. The initial stabilization efforts did not hold, however, and by 1985, Mexico was again experiencing severe economic difficulty and increasing tension with its creditors and the International Monetary Fund. The negotiation of a new IMF standby in July 1986 marked the resolution of these tensions.

This round of crisis and reconciliation led to important shifts within the Mexican administration. Economic difficulties had already strengthened the hand of the technocrats within the administration, but their views about the relationship between stabilization and structural reform began to shift, and the stabilization efforts of 1985–86 were accompanied by the initiation of trade reform and negotiations that led to accession to GATT. In the Solidarity Pact of 1988, which was designed to address a third cycle of macroeconomic difficulties, the government used the much-needed stabilization program to counter strong resistance from the private sector to further trade policy reform. The government cut the maximum tariff level from 100 percent to 20 percent, the average tariff level dropped to just over 10 percent, and most licensing requirements outside of the energy and transport sector fell.[8] By the time the Salinas administration took office in 1989, the trade reform had largely been completed.

In the late 1980s and early 1990s, trade liberalization accelerated in Latin America, but often not before macroeconomic mismanage-

---

7. See Kaufman, Bazdresch, and Herredia (1994, pp. 390–96); Pastor and Wise (1994).
8. See Lustig (1992, p. 118–19).

ment had contributed to a new round of balance of payments problems, accelerating inflation, and a reversal of earlier liberalization efforts. Argentina began reducing tariffs in 1988, but it was not until the failed Alfonsin government left office in July 1989 and stabilization was initiated by his successor, Peronist Saul Menem, that trade reform came onto the agenda in a serious way. The major reform occurred in 1991 when the country adopted a three-tier tariff scheme with rates ranging from 0 percent to 22 percent. The government also eliminated virtually all licensing requirements except for autos.[9] A similar pattern is visible in Peru. The Fujimori administration entered office in the midst of a crisis and not only stabilized but dramatically reduced the average tariff level. It also virtually eliminated quantitative restrictions and established a two-tier tariff system with rates at 15 percent and 25 percent.[10]

The pattern of mismanagement leading to a new government that undertakes radical reform is also visible in Venezuela.[11] The 1983 debt crisis in Venezuela initially led to an even more complex and restrictive set of controls than had existed in the past. An expansionist adjustment strategy in 1986–88 left the country with profound balance of payments and fiscal problems. Trade liberalization began in earnest with a change of government that brought an unlikely reformer to office, Carlos Andres Perez. The new government combined a difficult stabilization program with radical trade reform.

Brazil has had one of the most protectionist trade regimes in the region as well as an aggressive industrial policy. Not surprisingly, it has moved more cautiously in liberalizing trade than have the other major Latin American countries and has come into grave conflict with the United States. In 1988 Brazil was one of three countries targeted by the United States for Super 301 action on the basis of its prohibition on imports of more than one thousand items and its highly restrictive licensing regime. At the core of that dispute was the broader issue of Brazil's insistence on "special and differential" treatment under GATT, and particularly the U.S. claim that the country was abusing article XVIII:B to maintain quantitative restrictions. Initial

9. See U.S. International Trade Commission (1992, p. 7–7).
10. See Wise (1994).
11. See Naim (1993, pp. 45–58). The one interesting exception to this pattern is Colombia, which undertook a major trade reform in 1990–91 in the absence of a manifest crisis. See U.S. International Trade Commission (1992, p. 6–9).

bilateral discussions with the United States produced little progress on resolving the dispute, partly because of the profound uncertainties surrounding the presidential election in Brazil, which contributed to the explosion of hyperinflation in 1989.

With the election of Fernando Color de Melo in December of that year, Brazilian policy changed dramatically. By mid-1990 the new government had undertaken a radical reform effort that linked a stabilization initiative with various structural adjustment measures. The trade reform virtually eliminated quantitative restrictions, with the controversial exception of the informatics industry. On the basis of these initial moves, the United States terminated the Super 301 action.[12] A 1991 four-year duty reduction plan aimed to cut the weighted average duty rate from 32 percent to 14.2 percent, though ongoing efforts to protect the country's capital goods sector became an important point of controversy in completing the Mercosur agreement in 1994.[13]

The pattern of reforms of the rules governing foreign direct investment in the region is broadly similar to the pattern of trade liberalization, though policy changes in this area have been more incremental and cautious and several restrictions remain in place.[14] Shortly after coming to office amid severe economic crisis, the Pinochet government promulgated a new foreign investment law, Decree Law 600, in 1974. The law, seeking to reestablish investor confidence in the aftermath of the Allende government, opened virtually all sectors of the economy to foreign participation and moved toward the extension of national treatment.[15] Though Chile still imposes some time restrictions on the repatriation of profits, it maintains a highly open investment regime.

Mexico's opening toward foreign direct investment was more gradual than its liberalization of trade but also confirms the importance of external shocks and concerns about investor confidence.[16] In 1973, during the mildly populist Echeverria administration and at the onset of the borrowing boom, the Mexican government consolidated its

12. See U.S. International Trade Commission (1992, pp. 7–14, 7–15).
13. See John Barham and Patrick McCurry, "Mercosur Four Limp to Customs Union Signing," *Financial Times*, August 5, 1994, p. 4.
14. For an overview see Baker and Holmes (1991).
15. See U.S. International Trade Commission (1992, pp. 5–14).
16. See Hufbauer and Schott (1992, p. 76).

rules governing foreign investment and technology transfer in a more restrictive direction. Foreign investment laws generally limited foreign participation to a maximum of 49 percent, established tighter restrictions or outright bans in other sectors, and established a national commission to screen all applications. A technology transfer law imposed standards and prior registration requirements for patents, trademarks, and technological services and established a second commission for reviewing and approving all licensing agreements. A central feature of this regulatory structure was great discretion: the commissions operated on the basis of extremely broad and permissive guidelines concerning the conditions under which applications could be accepted or rejected and the terms on which investments and licensing would be done.

Following the debt crisis of August 1982, the government's stance became more accommodating. In 1984 Mexico issued new guidelines for the promotion of foreign investment that allowed majority ownership in certain activities. Though foreign investment increased rapidly after new debt servicing agreements were reached in 1987, it did not respond in the magnitude the government felt was needed. In 1988 automatic approval was granted to investments of up to 49 percent in established firms, but it was under the new Salinas government that foreign investment became a priority. In May 1989 the government issued more extensive reforms in the regulations governing the implementation of the foreign investment law. The new regulations did not scrap the 1973 law outright and maintained a complicated structure that included "classified" activities that carried various restrictions. But the policy also opened unclassified activities to 100 percent foreign control and automatic approval; by one estimate, the unclassified sectors covered approximately two-thirds of Mexican gross domestic product.[17]

Argentina's liberalization of foreign direct investment laws was a component of the sweeping Emergency Economic Law (EEL) passed in the early days of the Menem government that was designed to address the country's hyperinflation. The EEL granted national treatment to foreign investors, lifted all general restrictions on capital remittance and capital repatriation, and opened most sectors to foreign participation.[18] In 1993 further reforms of the foreign investment

17. See Hufbauer and Schott (1992, p. 77).
18. See U.S. International Trade Commission (1992, pp. 7–9).

law provided the basis for the negotiation of a bilateral investment treaty with the United States that went even further than the 1989 reforms: national treatment or most favored nation status, whichever is superior; free transfer of profits, capital, and royalties; abolition of all performance requirements; and allowance of international arbitration.[19]

Investment in the Andean Pact countries had been governed since 1971 by Decision 24, a statute designed to establish multilateral control over investment in the region through a restrictive common investment code. In April 1991 the Andean countries repealed Decision 24, replacing it with a new statute that equalized tax and fiscal incentives, eliminated restrictions on capital gains and profit remittances, and eliminated the burdensome requirement that foreign firms form joint ventures in order to establish or market within the region. However, before these reforms, existing national restrictions had fallen in all of the Andean member countries. Bolivia, Colombia, and Venezuela undertook major reforms of their investment laws in 1990–91 that anticipated the move toward national treatment and greater freedom of investors to repatriate profits and capital.

The reform movement in Latin America was not limited to stabilization, trade liberalization, and changes in the rules that directly governed the activities of foreign investors, such as sectoral restrictions, joint venture requirements, or the ability to repatriate profits and capital. Rather, the reforms extended to a variety of "behind-the-border" regulatory changes as well. Of course, these policy changes had important domestic motivations, but they are germane to a discussion of deep integration because they typically involved conformity with emerging multilateral rules under negotiation via GATT, explicit bilateral coordination, typically with the United States, or unilateral alignment with foreign norms and practices.

Privatization provides an important example. The principal motives for privatizing centered on the fiscal drain posed by loss-making enterprises and the presumed inefficiencies associated with public ownership. However, privatization has generally been accompanied— if not effected—by substantial foreign participation.[20] Moreover, foreign participation has hinged on significant regulatory reforms in the major privatized sectors such as telecommunications, electric power,

19. See Hufbauer and Schott (1994, p. 58).
20. See Petrazinni (1993).

and the airlines. This process of deregulation did not imply convergence around a single international norm; as Mark S. Fowler and Aileen Amarandos Pisciotta show for the telecommunications industry, there are many different models among the advanced industrial states that Latin American governments might adopt.[21] But privatization did imply adjustments designed to accommodate the interests of foreign firms and of the home governments that have become increasingly aggressive in backing them.

Unlike liberalization of trade and foreign investment, privatization is an ongoing process that will take years to complete. Only a brief overview of the initiation of reform efforts can be provided here.[22] Chile, again, was the pioneer, launching its original initiative in 1974. The drive to privatize was interrupted by the crisis of the early 1980s but resumed in force after 1985, fueled by an aggressive use of debt-equity swaps. The Mexican government was initially much more cautious. Total privatizations between 1983 and 1988 were limited to smaller enterprises, but the momentum shifted thereafter, leading up to the immensely successful privatization of 46 percent of government shares of Teléfonos de México in 1990–91. By 1993 Chile and Mexico had privatized about 90 percent of all state-owned enterprises, though the government maintained its control over the largest natural resource enterprises: CODELCO in Chile and PEMEX in Mexico.[23] In Argentina, privatization was another component of the government's macroeconomic adjustment efforts; privatization began in 1991 with the sale of the state telephone company and the national airlines. Like Argentina, Peru began its privatization scheme in 1991 in the wake of hyperinflation, and Venezuela's gained steam in that year with the sale of the national airline. Predictably, Brazil's privatization got off to a slow start in 1990 and faced political obstacles, first in the form of demonstrations against the sale of a major steel firm, later as a result of hesitancy on the part of the government. Foreign participation was also more limited than in the other countries. In 1992, however, the pace of privatization in Brazil began to quicken.

As in East Asia, changes in intellectual property protection offer an example of deep integration under pressure. As appendix B shows,

---

21. Fowler and Pisciotta (1993).
22. For overviews, see Boeker (1993); World Bank (1993a, pp. 77–96).
23. World Bank (1993a, p. 77).

many countries in the region have undertaken reforms in this area, and securing needed foreign investment in technology-intensive areas is clearly the underlying motivation. However, almost all of the major Latin American countries have run afoul of the United States on intellectual property issues, and the negotiation of the Uruguay Round provisions on intellectual property have undoubtedly helped define national positions on the issue. The main difficulties—most visible in Argentina and Brazil—have been political ones in securing domestic legislation.

Policy reforms affecting the service sector, particularly financial services, are a final example of the intertwining of domestically driven reform efforts and the processes of international coordination associated with deep integration. The longer-term objective of increasing the efficiency of the financial sector and short-term financial crises have contributed to efforts at reforming financial markets in the region since the late 1970s and even earlier. Argentina, Chile, Colombia, Uruguay, and Venezuela undertook liberalizing measures at that time, and Brazil initiated a substantial reform after 1964.

Beginning in the late 1980s, however, both implicit and explicit coordination have influenced the reform process and are likely to matter more seriously in the future because of multilateral and regional initiatives. First, regulatory reform of the financial sector and capital markets sought to maximize access to new commercial lending and the growth of portfolio investment from the advanced industrial states to the "emerging markets." Brazil, Colombia, Mexico, Peru, and Venezuela initiated reforms in the past five years to ease the entry of portfolio investment. Financial services are also the central component of the follow-up negotiations to the GATT round that began in 1994. The United States, whose banks and brokers stand to gain substantially from the opening of Latin America's financial sector, has a long-standing interest in the matter. Financial services are also likely to be a component of any discussion of regional integration, as an analysis of Mexico and NAFTA makes clear.

Mexico and NAFTA

If one excludes the European Community's absorption of Spain, Portugal, and Greece, NAFTA is the one deep integration scheme in

the world that unites developed and developing countries.[24] To understand why the agreement took the form it did, the political economy
of reform within Mexico must be understood. NAFTA would have
been impossible if Mexico had not already been launched on a path
of dramatic economic reform.

However, the international political dimension of the process
was also important. First, the template of the U.S.-Canada Free
Trade Agreement exerted a powerful influence over the NAFTA
negotiations, and that agreement contained several deep integration measures.[25] If NAFTA accession is to be the route toward
hemispheric integration, any subsequent negotiations between the
United States and other Latin American countries will have to
build on NAFTA. Second, the final shape of NAFTA was determined by a complex two-level game in which Mexico was called
upon to make concessions to appease domestic opponents in the
United States. These concessions centered on the environment and
labor standards and exemplify the new issues that are likely to
dominate the deep integration agenda for the developing countries
in the future (see appendix C).

Though Canada differs in several obvious and important respects from developing countries in the hemisphere, Canada's high
level of dependence on the United States and the politically significant nationalist political forces in the country offer an interesting
comparison with Mexico.[26] In the negotiation of the U.S.-Canada
Free Trade Agreement (FTA), the two sides had different political
objectives. American trade officials consistently stressed the legal
compatibility of the agreement with GATT and emphasized that
the pursuit of free trade with Canada in no way signaled a reduced
commitment to multilateralism. At the same time, however, officials pointed out that the inclusion of new issues could serve as a
precedent or model for the expansion of the GATT negotiations to

24. The literature on NAFTA is vast, but for assessments from different perspectives,
see Lustig, Bosworth, and Lawrence (1992); Grinspun and Cameron (1993); Hufbauer
and Schott (1992). A useful guide to the final agreement is Hufbauer and Schott (1993).

25. Not surprisingly, President Bush's announcement of the intention to negotiate a
free trade agreement with Mexico in June 1990 was followed in February 1991, at Canada's
insistence, by an expansion of the talks into a three-way negotiation for a North American
Free Trade Agreement.

26. For two useful discussions of the underlying factors behind Canada's entry, see
Winham (1988) and Wonnacott (1991).

incorporate deep integration issues, including especially services and investment.[27]

Bilateral negotiations with a powerful trading partner in the absence of established rules run certain risks for small countries; nationalist opposition to the agreement in Canada was intense. Yet a powerful political compact with the United States also had appeal to Canada and Mexico. Such an agreement would reduce the risk from congressional and administrative actions by establishing clear rules and a mechanism for dispute settlement that would limit American discretion. Canadian concerns about dispute resolution were reenforced during the negotiations when the United States took several legally questionable trade actions against Canada.[28] The creation of a bilateral dispute settlement mechanism, the Canada-U.S. Trade Commission, was thus a major objective of the Canadians.

The politics of the passage of the U.S.-Canada Free Trade Agreement was remarkably smooth in the United States. The politics of NAFTA, by contrast, was tempestuous.

Even though George Bush had made freer trade with Mexico a campaign issue in 1988, the administration believed it was crucial that the Salinas administration move first.[29] It was first learned through a press leak that Mexico was seeking an FTA with the United States in March 1990.[30] Preliminary discussions began during the summer of 1990, the trade ministers of the two countries made the joint recommendation to begin formal negotiations on August 8, and on August 21, President Salinas requested that the ratification process

27. See, for example, statement of Allan Wallis, Under Secretary of State for Economic Affairs. U.S. Congress (1988, p. 13).

28. The most significant were the 1986 softwood lumber cases, in which the U.S. industry obtained a ruling that Canadian stumpage practices were a countervailable subsidy, the 1987 shakes and shingles case, in which the U.S. industry obtained safeguards protection, and the controversy about Canada's Western Grain Transport Act, which the United States argued constituted an export subsidy for western wheat growers.

29. The administration did take several small measures to reward Salinas for his unilateral trade actions. In October 1989, the United States doubled Mexico's quota under the steel VRA, and in early 1990 the United States agreed to increase significantly its quotas on imports of textiles and apparel in response to Mexico's elimination of quotas on these products. In 1990 the United States granted extremely generous GSP concessions to Mexico that covered $2 billion worth of exports.

30. See Lustig (1992, p. 132).

be conducted under fast-track rules. On September 25, 1990, Bush notified Congress of his intention to negotiate an FTA with Mexico, and the politics of NAFTA began in earnest.

A coalition of labor and specific industries mobilized against the agreement. The AFL-CIO opposed NAFTA vociferously, supported by the textile industry and certain agricultural interests, including dairy, sugar, peanuts, citrus, and tomatoes. Battle lines were drawn as much on regional as partisan or sectoral grounds. Legislators from manufacturing states in the industrial heartland joined with farm and textile representatives to oppose the agreement, while the administration secured support from the coasts and the southwestern border states.

Given that the American market was already open, the concerns of the opposition centered as much on the anticipated effects of the agreement on investment flows as they did on the further liberalization of trade. Labor revived arguments about the threat of "runaway shops," fears fueled by Ross Perot's catchy but misguided prediction that the passage of NAFTA would be accompanied by a "giant sucking sound" as American plants and jobs fled south to the lower wage and weakly regulated labor markets of Mexico.[31]

Environmental groups also cast their opposition in terms of the effect of the agreement on investment. They pointed to the poor record of the border industries and argued that U.S. environmental standards would come under pressure or be circumvented if firms could relocate across the border, where standards are weaker.

Supporting the agreement was a formidable array of business interests; investment was a major preoccupation of these groups, and their demands help account for the deep integration measures that constitute the most innovative components of NAFTA (see appendix C). Almost all of the major umbrella organizations representing big business, including the National Association of Manufacturers, the National Retail Federation, the Business Roundtable, and the United States Council for International Business, expressed support for granting the president both negotiating authority and the fast track. Interestingly, support for the agreement came not only from Fortune

---

31. For an overview of the political arguments against NAFTA, see Perot and Choate (1993). For a refutation of their claims concerning job losses, see Hufbauer and Schott (1993, pp. 173–77).

500 companies but also from the small- and medium-sized businesses grouped in the Chamber of Commerce. These organizations were joined by free-trade lobbies (the National Foreign Trade Council, the Emergency Committee for American Trade) and a variety of business organizations with specific interests in Mexico.[32]

For both advocates and opponents of NAFTA, issues of deep integration were central. For the business backers of NAFTA, the agreement offered new investment opportunities in Mexico and a chance to improve the overall climate of conducting business. The nontrade components of NAFTA were explicitly aimed at improving the investment climate, not only by lifting existing restrictions but by extending various guarantees, for example, on the availability of foreign exchange, expropriation, and dispute settlement (see appendix B). For opponents, the absence of adequate convergence became the rallying cry; environmental standards became the battleground.

The dependence of the Bush administration on congressional approval of fast-track procedures provided the crucial opening for critics to expand the NAFTA agenda. In March 1991 House Ways and Means Committee Chairman Dan Rostenkowski and Senate Finance Committee Chairman Lloyd Bentsen wrote U.S. Trade Representative Carla Hills, arguing that lawmakers would want any Mexican agreement to include provisions on labor's right to organize, health and safety standards in the workplace, and environmental laws. On May 1 the Bush administration responded to congressional pressures by presenting a 150-page "action plan" for the negotiation of the free trade agreement with Mexico. The plan contained several significant concessions. Besides additional spending for worker retraining, the administration promised to pursue an agreement with Mexico on labor standards and their enforcement. The plan countered environmental opposition through a combination of concessions and co-optation. The plan included commitments that the agreement would not be allowed to erode environmental standards in the United States. A representative of an environmental organization would hold a seat on the U.S. Trade Representative's Advisory Committee on Trade Policy and Negotiations, as well as on lower-level trade advisory groups. It

---

32. Including the American Chamber of Commerce of Mexico, the Coalition for North American Trade and Investment, the Mexico-U.S. Business Committee, and the U.S.-Mexico Chamber of Commerce.

also promised the creation of a North American Environmental Commission.

The administration's action plan had the crucial effect of swinging the vote of Richard Gephardt and the twenty to thirty Democrats he was able to carry with him. In retrospect, the closeness of the final vote suggests that the action plan was probably decisive in securing congressional passage of fast-track provisions. Nonetheless, the final vote on the fast track was much closer than expected and suggests the differences in the politics that are likely to characterize North-North versus North-South deep integration agreements. In 1988 nine senators and forty representatives voted against the Canadian agreement. In 1991 the vote on granting the president fast-track authority—virtually a referendum on the U.S.-Mexico agreement—was 231–192 in the House and 59–36 in the Senate.

Though the Bush administration succeeded in securing passage of the fast-track provisions for the U.S.-Mexico free trade agreement in May 1991 and concluding the negotiations with Mexico before leaving office, the Clinton administration faced the difficult task of securing NAFTA's passage. This task was complicated because the agreement was implicated in the complex three-way 1992 presidential election, in which independent candidate Ross Perot campaigned vigorously against NAFTA. Promises that Clinton made during the election campaign to improve the agreement with respect to labor standards and the environment once again allowed skeptics to broaden the NAFTA agenda and guaranteed that further negotiations would have to be conducted with Mexico, even if the NAFTA text itself was not to be reopened.

The debate is germane to the question of deep integration, because it centered precisely on the powers that would be granted to a newly created North American Commission on the Environment. Initially, the Clinton administration favored a consultative forum, partly because of concern that U.S. laws could be held accountable under a supranational mechanism.[33] However, under pressure from environmental and labor groups and Democrats in Congress, and facing stiff Mexican resistance to the inclusion of new substantive commitments, the administration gradually moved toward the creation of two complex dispute settlement structures that were given powers to oversee

---

33. See "Confidential Options Paper Signals Likely Dismissal of Clinton Surge Pledge," *Inside U.S. Trade*, March 12, 1993, pp. 1, 11–14.

the enforcement of national environmental and labor laws. These bodies would have the power, under highly restrictive conditions, to levy fines and even invoke trade sanctions to guarantee that national laws were enforced (see appendix C). Mexico initially objected that such a structure would constitute an unwarranted violation of national sovereignty; the American business community also objected to the use of trade sanctions as a mechanism of enforcement.[34] But as it became clear that the entire NAFTA was hostage to the side agreements, Mexico capitulated on all issues, including the most contentious one of trade sanctions. Only with these agreements in place was Clinton able to secure passage by a narrow margin in November 1993.

In sum, the U.S. position on deeper integration sprang from government efforts to accommodate the interests of both the supporters and opponents of the agreement. What were Mexico's interests in accepting such a wide-ranging agenda?

The chronology is important. The de la Madrid and Salinas administrations had at least initiated almost all of the reforms that were later incorporated into NAFTA. Trade reform began in mid-1985 and was already consolidated by 1988. In 1986 Mexico joined GATT following discussions with the United States on the terms of its accession. The reforms in the investment regime began very soon after the debt crisis but were pushed further in 1989. Intellectual property reforms began in 1987, and the main decision to expand protection had been taken by January 1990. Between 1989 and 1990, the government independently launched a series of deregulation initiatives: in finance, road transport, petrochemicals, telecommunications, sugar, mining, and fishing.[35] As was suggested, this pattern of reform was motivated by crisis and changing views of the relationship between stabilization and structural adjustment within the economic bureaucracy. The capacity of the government to initiate and sustain these reforms must be attributed in no small measure to the dominance and strong hand of the ruling party.

However, the Mexican administration had two further motives for the agreement. First, even though trade between the two countries

34. See "Major Business Groups Signal Opposition to U.S. Drafts on NAFTA Side Pacts," *Inside U.S. Trade*, June 4, 1993, pp. 1, 12–13.

35. See Lustig (1992, pp. 108–11).

was relatively free, Mexico, like Canada, was the victim of a number of bilateral trade actions in the late 1980s.[36] Moreover, like Canada, the country was highly dependent on the United States; in 1989 the United States accounted for nearly 70 percent of both imports and exports. The agreement thus provided a way of securing access to the North American market and an institutionalized mechanism for managing bilateral disputes.

Second, the agreement served an important domestic political function, one that is likely to be germane for other nations throughout the hemisphere as integration experiments expand. In undertaking reforms, governments in countries with a volatile policy history face a political dilemma. Most reforms are technically reversible, and the combination of reputation and underlying political support that engenders confidence emerges only over time; in short, establishing credibility is a problem. Yet for a reform program to hold, investment must respond aggressively to new incentives. Though foreign investment in Mexico increased rapidly after 1987, it did not respond as hoped. Salinas was reported to have been especially discouraged by a trip to Europe that revealed a preoccupation with developments in Central Europe and a lack of interest in, or knowledge about, the depth of the Mexican reforms.[37]

In the face of this dilemma, one would expect governments to seek additional ways of assuring investors by signaling the seriousness and irreversibility of policies. One such means is through institutional changes that increase the cost of policy reversal. Thus a political leader seeking to assure investors will not only change policies but will delegate authority to agencies that are likely to pursue the desired policies in the future. This process of delegation might occur by increasing the powers and independence of particular government agencies, such as the central bank and ministry of finance. However, a similar function can be performed by signing international agreements, especially agreements such as NAFTA, which provide institutional means for oversight and enforcement. Thus although dispute settlement mechanisms are designed in part to restrain the United States, they must also be seen as devices for restraining Mexico and thus signaling its intent.

---

36. Erzan and Yeats (1992), for example, find that Mexico was more vulnerable to administrative trade actions and nontrivial (that is, greater than 5 percent) tariffs than was any other country in the region.

37. See Pastor (1990).

A Hemispheric Initiative?

At roughly the same time that the United States and Mexico were beginning discussions on NAFTA, President Bush made the wholly unexpected announcement on June 27, 1990, of his Enterprise for the Americas Initiative (EAI). The new initiative rested on three pillars: investment promotion, aid via debt reduction, and the elimination of trade barriers. The investment component of the package signaled U.S. interests toward the region clearly: its major objective was the liberalization of rules governing foreign direct investment through the initiation of two new programs to be administered through the Inter-American Development Bank.[38] The debt provisions of the initiative contain more relief than was initially extended under the Brady plan.[39] As with the Brady plan, however, the extension of relief would also hinge on a large dose of conditionality: the country must have an IMF standby and World Bank SAL or SECAL in place; the country must undertake a liberalization of its investment regime in line with the investment portion of the initiative; and the country should have reached agreement with its commercial creditors.

The centerpiece of the new initiative and its greatest departure from past policy, however, were its provisions on trade. First, Bush offered closer cooperation with the Latin American countries in the Uruguay Round, including the promise to seek deeper tariff cuts in products of relevance to Latin America. Second, Bush announced that "the U.S. stands ready to enter into free trade agreements with other markets in Latin America and the Caribbean, particularly with groups of countries that have associated for purposes of trade liberalization."[40] Finally, given that such a step was likely to be too dramatic

38. The first would be a lending program akin to existing World Bank sector adjustment loans to provide technical assistance in the drafting of new investment codes. The second proposal was for a multilateral investment fund that would extend up to $300 million a year in grants in support of such liberalization and privatization efforts. The money for the fund would be supplied in equal $100 million amounts by Japan, the United States, and the European Community, though the administration hoped that additional commitments could expand the size of the fund to over $2 billion. See Hakim (1992).

39. The initiative would create a debt facility administered by Treasury empowered to provide new payment terms on foreign assistance, including P.L. 480 aid. Reduction or cancellation of Export-Import Bank and Commodity Credit Corporation loans was also to be allowed if the country used the relief for debt-for-equity or debt-for-nature swaps. Hakim (1992, 97–98).

40. See Bush (1991, p. 1011).

for some countries to consider, Bush also offered the negotiation of bilateral framework agreements that would permit more incremental negotiations covering particular issues.

The Enterprise for the Americas Initiative and NAFTA were not in any way linked at their inception, but the completion of NAFTA against the backdrop of a widespread move toward liberalization among the countries of the region began to raise important questions about how trade would be politically organized in the Western Hemisphere.[41] As in Asia, competing visions became apparent in the early 1990s, each with somewhat different implications for deeper integration in the hemisphere.[42]

Through the middle of 1994, most policy pronouncments coming from both the United States and Latin America focused on the NAFTA option for hemispheric integration. This model saw a gradual incorporation of more countries into NAFTA, with the implication that entering countries would be required to conform with the high standards of the existing agreement. This approach would essentially extend NAFTA's deep integration provisions to the rest of the hemisphere, beginning with countries such as Chile where economic reform was well advanced.

A second option was for the United States to negotiate bilateral FTAs, building on the earlier "framework agreements" that the United States negotiated with a number of countries in the wake of the announcment of the EAI. For the United States, such a strategy had a distinct advantage: it would take the provisions of NAFTA as a baseline, on top of which new demands would be added. For the Latin American countries, this was but one of several disadvantages of the bilateral model. Since agreements would be negotiated bilaterally, they would not necessarily imply closer political integration among the Latin American states themselves. It was precisely fear of such a hub-spoke outcome that led Canada to opt for full inclusion in the free trade negotiations with Mexico.

41. The timing of the initiative would appear to link it to developments with Mexico. Bush claimed, however, to have been influenced by a meeting held in February 1990 in Cartagena with the heads of state of three Andean countries, which led to a Treasury study of U.S. foreign economic policy toward the region. The following discussion of the initiative draws from the text of Bush's speech (Bush 1991).

42. I exclude from consideration purely preferential agreements, such as the Caribbean Basin Initiative or the Andean Trade Preference Act.

The third organizational option was to move toward a hemispheric free trade area all at once rather than through the sequential negotiations that would be required for NAFTA accession or bilateral FTAs. This option was ultimately endorsed by the Summit of the Americas, held in Miami in December 1994.

One motive for pursuing this third organizational option was to rationalize the increasingly complex patchwork of subregional integration initiatives and bilateral FTAs that were emerging among the Latin American countries, some of which were distinctly hostile to NAFTA or the prospect of bilateral FTAs with the United States. The explosion of such initiatives throughout the region since the early 1990s has been remarkable. A Southern Cone Common Market (Mercosur) between Argentina, Brazil, Uruguay, and Paraguay was signed in March 1991; shortly thereafter an agreement was signed between Mercosur and the United States. Despite difficult disagreements centering on Brazilian industrial policy, compromises on a common external tariff were reached in 1994, creating a large and powerful trading bloc.[43] At a meeting of the Andean Pact council in 1990, only the fifth since the organization's inception in 1969, the members endorsed the formation of a free trade area by 1992. By 1994 negotiations had advanced to the formation of a customs union.

The negotiation of subregional agreements, in turn, generated demand for bilateral deals between the new subregional agreements and interested third parties. Before the negotiation of NAFTA was even complete, Mexico had embarked on negotiations for free trade agreements with Chile and the Central American countries. In April 1991, Mexico announced that it would seek to establish a free trade zone with Venezuela and Colombia; the agreement among the so-called G-3 was signed in 1994.[44] Chile subsequently struck bilateral FTAs with Mexico, Colombia, and Venezuela and in 1994 was negotiating a relationship with Mercosur.

There were also emerging signs of interest within Latin America for merging these various efforts into a regionwide agreement "from below." In March 1994 Brazil called for the formation of a South American FTA. With its implication that the United States would, at

43. See Cardenas (1992); Dandeker (1992).
44. See "Group of Three Sign Free-Trade Accord while Andeans Agree on External Tariff," *Andean Group Report*, June 30, 1994, p. 1.

least initially, be excluded, the South American FTA idea bore an uncanny resemblance to the Malaysian proposal for an exclusive East Asian Economic Grouping. At a meeting in Cartagena, Colombia, in June 1994, the leaders of nineteen countries began initial discussions on how the emerging patchwork of agreements might be merged into a single, unified structure.[45]

The Clinton administration's postponement of the quest for fast-track authority in September 1994 severely dampened hopes that the Miami summit would yield a meaningful trade agreement; early American statements appeared to purposefully downplay the economic component of the agenda. Nonetheless, the Plan of Action ratified by the summit opted strongly for the hemispheric option by establishing a timetable for the negotiation of a Free Trade Area of the Americas (FTAA) by no later than 2005. Rather than creating a new institution, administrative support for the minsterial meetings was placed in the hands of the Special Committee on Trade of the Organization of American States.

Despite the apparent breakthrough of the Miami summit, crucial issues of both organizational design and substance remain to be solved. Despite the apparent commitment to the hemispheric option, it is not clear that the Miami summit resolved the conflict among the contending organizational designs outlined above. There are currently six major trade groups in the Western Hemisphere: NAFTA, Mercosur, the Andean Pact, the G-3, the Central American Common Market, and Caricom, which organizes thirteen English-language Caribbean countries. Among them, these agreements cover all countries in the hemisphere except for Cuba, the Dominican Republic, Haiti, Panama, and Suriname. However, it is not clear that these very different agreements can simply be merged, nor what the status of existing agreements would be under the new FTAA. These questions were muddied, rather than clarified, by the U.S. announcement on the last day of the summit that Chile would be invited to join the NAFTA. Was this a first step toward the FTAA, or was NAFTA moving on its own separate track?

Moreover, it is not clear exactly what issues will fall under the aegis of the new FTAA; the declaration of principles states that barriers to

45. James Brooke, *New York Times,* "Latins Envision a Single Trade Zone," June 17, 1994, p. D2.

trade and investment will be progressively eliminated but does not state whether that process will be limited to shallow integration measures or will embrace the deep integration agenda contained in NAFTA.[46] There are signs that hemispheric cooperation might evolve toward deeper integration. As a result of U.S. initiative, for example, the Plan of Action establishes a Committee on Hemispheric Financial Issues to examine steps to promote liberalization of capital movements and the progressive integration of capital markets.

Yet to seek an agreement among the diverse countries of the hemisphere on such issues is likely to result in outcomes that parallel those in Asia to a greater extent, including a weakening of the quest for a deep integration agreement for the whole hemisphere along the lines of NAFTA. As I will argue in the conclusion, NAFTA is more likely to constitute an anomaly than be the harbinger of future trends in deep integration between North and South.

46. Summit of the Americas, "Declaration of Principles," December 9–11, 1994, Miami, Fla., p. 2.

Chapter 5

The ACP States, the European Community Associates, and India

*T*HE deep integration agenda is more salient to the middle-income nations of East and Southeast Asia and Latin America than it is for most other developing nations. Issues such as intellectual property rights and competition policy are quite distant from the core policy concerns of poorer countries. Furthermore, the governments and firms of the advanced industrial states have no compelling reason to push such issues on them aggressively. The United States has been the advanced industrial state most intent on pushing deeper integration on developing countries, and U.S. economic interests in Asia and Latin America are far greater than they are in Africa, South Asia, or even the Middle East.

However, there are grounds for looking briefly at the African, Caribbean, and Pacific (ACP) states and the Mediterranean associates of the European Community (European Union). For both groups of countries, the special relationship with the EU constitutes the most important international institutional structure for their foreign economic policy. As with American and Japanese relations with the developing world, a "dialogue" over policy reform issues has become central. Moreover, the deeper integration of Europe through the 1992 process raises questions about the future relationship between the community and developing countries.

Though India is a low-income country when measured by GNP per capita, its large size, industrial base, and technological sophistication make several deep integration issues highly salient. India led the developing countries' unsuccessful resistance to the inclusion of several deep integration issues, particularly services and intellectual

100

property, in the Uruguay Round negotiations. Since that time, however, the country has undergone a domestic policy revolution that has strongly affected its foreign economic policy.

The ACP States and Mediterranean Associates

Since the inception of the European Development Fund in 1958, and through the Yaounde Conventions (1963 and 1969), the Community's aid program prided itself on a conception of equal partnership between the EC and the ACP states.[1] This partnership initially included strong principles of nondiscrimination and reciprocity, including the right of corporate establishment. In effect, the early vision of association was of bilateral free-trade agreements between the Community and each developing country partner.

Lomé I (1975), negotiated following British accession to the EC, reflected a subtle shift in the conception of the EC-ACP relationship, a shift that mirrored political pressures in the larger multilateral arena. With Lomé I, the EC moved to bring its aid efforts into greater conformity with third world demands for a new international economic order.[2] Two features of Lomé I are germane. First, the EC states made an explicit pledge not to attempt to influence the development models of the ACP states; second, at the insistence of the ACP countries, Lomé I abandoned the principle of reciprocal rights of establishment and did not include any guarantees on the security of foreign investment.

In a 1982 review of aid policy by the EC commissioner for development cooperation, Edgard Pisani, the winds began to shift.[3] Though reiterating the principle of partnership and explicitly rejecting a rigid conditionality, Pisani argued that the time had come "to extend the political dialogue beyond the mere negotiations on projects to be financed . . . [to] the effectiveness of the policies supported." Responding to critics of EC aid policy, the Pisani memorandum noted that past

1. For a history of the Yaounde conventions, see Zartman (1971).
2. These changes included greater emphasis on aid for industry, a commodity price stabilization agreement (STABEX), and an abandonment of the principle of reciprocity in favor of preferences. For a history of the Lomé conventions, see Ravenhill (1985).
3. The Pisani Report is contained in Commission of the European Communities (1982).

failures were partly the result of the shortcomings of the ACP states themselves: urban bias, preferences for large projects, and weak administration.[4] As Enzo Grilli notes, "The principle of neutrality of the Community with respect to ACP development strategies and priorities, while not reversed, was thus being narrowed in its practical sphere of application."[5]

The negotiation of Lomé III in 1984–85, at the height of the debt crisis, showed further evidence of these changes. Lomé III made several hortatory responses to ACP states' demands, but at EC insistence, the ACP group agreed in a joint statement to negotiate bilateral investment treaties that would extend guarantees to European firms. Lomé IV (1990) brought further shifts in EC aid policy, including an earmarking of a certain share of aid funds for structural adjustment (rather than project) purposes, a services chapter, and an explicit commitment to the development of the private sector. This last measure implied not only greater emphasis on the development of the domestic private sector but improved protection for foreign investment as well.[6]

Since 1989 EC policy toward the Mediterranean associates has shown similar concerns, though broader political issues have surfaced: how to strengthen ties between the EC and North Africa as an antidote to the rise of Islamic fundamentalism and attendant political instability.[7] Pushed by France, the initiation of the Euro-Maghreb partnership in 1992 aimed at this objective and sought to create a political dialogue, to deepen technical and cultural cooperation, and to begin the process of establishing a free trade area between the Maghreb and the EC. The initiative also contemplates the financing of technical assistance similar to that extended to the Central European countries and even supports the creation of a Euro-Maghreb development bank.[8] However, there has been little discussion of deep integration.

A comparison with the Eastern European countries shows that the pressure on the developing countries for deeper integration arising from the Lomé process or from the association agreements is mini-

4. Commission of the European Communities (1982, p. 16).
5. Grilli (1993, p. 112).
6. Cosgrove and Laurent (1992, pp. 127–33).
7. Grilli (1993, pp. 213–4).
8. See Sutton (1992).

mal. The agreements signed between the EC and Czechoslovakia, Hungary, and Poland in December 1991 covered an array of internal regulatory policies, including customs law, company law, banking law, company accounts and taxes, protection of workers in the workplace, protection of health and animals, technical rules and standards, and the environment. These agreements will mean that "the central European states design the legal foundations of their new economic system in accordance with the EC model."[9] Aid policy has placed some pressure on the ACP states and associates on questions of shallow integration. But outside of Turkey, the prospects for the entry of developing countries into the EC are nil, and thus few incentives exist for fundamental policy adjustments that would lead to deeper integration. Despite signs of a gradual expansion of aid conditionality, the Lomé and associate relationships remain essentially preferential ones in which little is demanded of the partners who are developing countries.

A second concern for the developing countries centers not on the direct effects of their relations with the Community, but on the possible indirect effects of the 1992 exercise. Much apprehension has focused on traditional trade issues, such as the consequences of the elimination or reduction of the current hodgepodge of national quantitative restrictions and the potential for trade diversion.[10]

But as the discussion of NAFTA showed, deeper regional integration among one group of countries can have effects on those outside it in other ways than trade diversion or explicit pressures for convergence. Policy convergence at higher standards than those currently in place can adversely affect existing preferential arrangements or produce what might be called "regulatory trade and investment diversion" by favoring the more advanced developing countries over the less advanced.[11] These questions have been raised in the Europe 1992

9. Kramer (1993, p. 229).

10. On the question of quantitative restrictions see Davenport (1990). The problem of trade diversion has two dimensions: the potential for diversion away from the ACP states toward Europe as 1992 proceeds but also the ongoing problem of the suppression of trade coming from non-ACP developing countries as a result of European preferences. In a recent dispute, for example, non-ACP banana producers complained that they were disadvantaged by European preferences extended to ACP producers. On East Asia's fears, see Han (1992).

11. Collaboration on standards might still be discriminatory against the developing country (or any outsider) even if the regime is based on mutual recognition. The developing

movement with reference to several standards issues, from plant and animal health standards that affect primary product exports to labeling and testing of manufactured exports. The conflict over the labeling of tropical timber, in which more lax European countries have been pressed to adopt the tougher labeling standards of the "greener" European countries, is a recent example.[12]

As Sheila Page has argued, the problem is not simply one of holding developing countries to unrealistic standards; the issues are also procedural and institutional.[13] As the community moves in fits and starts toward ever-deeper integration, it will become more important for developing countries to have access to the standard-setting process and be able to obtain timely information about new decisions. In this small sense, Europe 1992 could have implications for the deeper integration of the ACP developing countries.

India

If the deep integration agenda has to date had little relevance for the ACP states, or even for the Mediterranean associates, the same cannot be said about India. The country's highly restrictive trade and investment regime, large domestic market, growing importance in world trade, and political role in leading third world resistance to the Uruguay Round have combined to make the country a target of external pressures, especially from the United States. India, with Japan and Brazil, was the target of the first U.S. Super 301 action, focused on insurance, and recurrent complaints about intellectual property protection.

There is little evidence that these pressures had much influence on Indian policy, however. Size and political alignments made the country relatively immune to reform, and tepid efforts at policy change under Rajiv Gandhi were overwhelmed by political resistance. Rather,

country exporter would still have to satisfy the requirements of at least one member state, which would require tests and certification and run the risk of "bureaucratic protectionism." See Davenport (1990, p. 194).

12. See Davenport (1990); Matthews and McAleese (1990). On the tropical timber issue, see Jean-Pierre Kiekens, "Towards Eco-Labelling of Tropical Timber," *Courier* (General Secretariat of the ACP Group of States, Brussels), no. 142 (November-December 1993), pp. 95–96.

13. Page (1992).

a combination of mounting fiscal difficulties, increasing inflation, external economic shocks, and domestic political changes spurred reforms. The external shocks came in the form of the Iraqi invasion of Kuwait, which cut off $2 billion in annual remittances from Indians working in the Persian Gulf, and the collapse of the Soviet Union, which had constituted an important export market and a source of cheap crude oil. The political changes began with the defeat of the ruling Congress party in 1989, a series of weak opposition governments, the assassination of Rajiv Gandhi during the May 1991 election campaign, and the formation of a new minority Congress government under P. V. Narasimha Rao in June.

The Rao government did not appear to be well positioned to initiate a reform program, let alone a bold one. However, the government inherited a completely unsustainable fiscal and balance of payments position and the virtual collapse of foreign confidence. The outgoing government had already initiated talks with the International Monetary Fund and signed a standby in January 1991; further reforms provided the basis for a second standby in September. With support from the IMF, the new government implemented reforms designed to stabilize the economy, including a massive tax reform. Yet as in Latin America, stabilization and structural adjustment were linked and spilled over into questions of deep integration.

One of the new government's first targets was the country's complex industrial policy.[14] A new industrial policy effectively dismantled an extraordinarily complex domestic licensing system and thus eliminated most government controls over investment and production decisions. The government did not couple these reforms with an aggressive privatization program that involved total divestiture, but it has sought substantial public sector reform through partial (up to 49 percent) divestiture, the introduction of a hard budget constraint, and financial support to close loss-making state-owned enterprises. In 1992 the government also began to tackle the problem of financial market reform through gradual interest rate liberalization, the licensing of new private sector banks to compete with the state-owned ones, and fundamental reforms of the regulatory apparatus governing the capital markets.

14. The following summary draws on Khalizadeh-Shirazi and Zagha (1994); Thomas (1994); Ahluwalia (1994).

The industrial policy reforms would have made little sense, however, in the absence of an aggressive program to reverse the highly restrictive regime governing trade and investment; shallow integration was the natural complement of domestic deregulation. The new policy opened many previously closed sectors to foreign direct investment and introduced automatic approval for all investments up to 51 percent of equity in many sectors.[15] The government further liberalized foreign investment in January 1993 by amending the 1973 Foreign Exchange Regulation Act (FERA). The act placed a host of complicated restrictions on the operations of companies with more than 40 percent foreign equity. The 1993 reform eliminated the discriminatory treatment of FERA companies and liberalized the rules on profit and dividend remittance. The amendment also liberalized restrictions on foreign equity, permitting 100 percent foreign ownership in export-oriented activities and selected sectors.

These domestic policy changes naturally affected India's larger foreign economic policy stance. By 1993, for example, the investment reforms allowed India to sign the convention of the Multilateral Investment Guarantee Agency and to initiate discussions on bilateral investment treaties.[16]

Trade policy followed suit. In 1992 the government officially replaced the Imports and Exports Act, which dated to 1947, and began a radical overhaul of the trade regime. Almost all raw materials and capital goods could be imported without a license. Tariff levels, which had been among the highest in the world, fell sharply, especially on capital goods and machinery. However, the crucial reform affecting trade was probably the liberalization of exchange rate management, which created an automatic mechanism for allocating foreign exchange.

These shallow integration measures have not translated unambiguously into an acceptance of the deep integration agenda. India's resistance on issues such as services and intellectual property was not simply a matter of principle; the largely state-owned service sector naturally resisted a greater foreign presence in sectors such as insurance. India's pharmaceutical companies have long profited from pi-

---

15. For a detailed analysis of all aspects of the investment climate, see Economist Intelligence Unit (1993).

16. See Roy (1993).

racy and have attempted to enlist the support of a farm lobby by raising fears that committing to GATT rules on intellectual property would entail losses to farmers because of the protection it would extend to certain bioengineered seed varieties. Moreover, the government has faced broader ideological resistance from the nationalist left over the involvement of the IMF and GATT in domestic decision-making.[17]

There is no regional organization that provides an international focal point pressing for these reforms as there is for Latin America. The countries of the South Asian Association for Regional Cooperation[18] have agreed to the establishment of a South Asian Preferential Trading Arrangement, but India is the leader rather than follower in this institution, and in any case its members account for only a tiny share of India's total trade: 2 percent in fiscal year 1991–92.[19] The chief international organizational locus of any deep integration efforts will thus center on India's gradual incorporation into the multilateral system, as well as on bilateral agreements with major partners. The United States has continued to press India on several issues, especially intellectual property rights, and suspended some GSP trade in 1992 to that end.[20]

However, the main battle lines are likely to be fought within India around the GATT agreement, which is currently being debated. As with other countries that have undertaken radical reforms, the internal political balance will in the end be determined by aggregate economic performance and the emergence of new interests—for example, in India's technology-intensive and export-oriented industries—that are amenable to deeper integration.[21]

---

17. See "The Lure of India," *Economist*, February 26, 1994, p. 33, and "Seeds of Discord," *Economist*, April 2, 1994, p. 36.

18. India, Bangladesh, Bhutan, Maldives, Pakistan, Nepal, and Sri Lanka.

19. Economist Intelligence Unit (1993, p. 10).

20. U.S. Trade Representative (1994, p. 122).

21. See Hamish McDonald, "The Late Convert," *Far Eastern Economic Review*, December 5, 1991, 64–5.

Chapter 6

Conclusion

MOST analyses of deep integration—including those in the Brookings Integrating National Economies project—view international cooperation as a response to the externalities created by closer economic ties. Cooperation may fail to materialize because of collective action problems, but the underlying assumption is that joint gains can be realized from more extensive policy coordination as interdependence increases. This belief suggests a developmental theory of deep integration: as countries reach a certain stage of development, level of economic integration with the world economy, and policy convergence, the demand for formal coordination increases.

Some evidence exists for this hypothesis. As this book suggests, the more advanced developing countries are the ones for which the deep integration agenda has become most salient. Clearly, negotiations over deeper integration that include the developing countries are less far advanced than those among the advanced industrial states, and nowhere are they as advanced as in Europe. Yet if a somewhat more expansive definition of deep integration is used, particularly by considering the reform of laws governing foreign direct investment and the spillover from such reforms into other regulatory changes, then signs of the deeper integration of the advanced developing countries are widespread, indeed ubiquitous, among the middle-income developing countries.

As this book shows, however, I believe that the benign view of the process of deep integration as the result of a natural course of growth, policy convergence, and mutually beneficial policy coordination overlooks the international and domestic politics of the process. First I have emphasized that the deep integration of the developing countries must be understood in the context of strong external pressures. The debt and balance of payments crises of the 1980s changed the bargaining power of the developing countries in comparison with their creditors and the international financial institutions. Domestic policy failures have been the major driving force behind the reform efforts of the 1980s and 1990s. But the need to restore creditworthiness, attract foreign investment, and secure multilateral finance has also exercised a strong influence over the substantive direction of developing country economic policy, especially for the regulatory issues that are the core of the deep integration agenda.

The developing countries have also faced direct political pressures in the past decade for deep integration, what Miles Kahler has called "harmonization through leverage."[1] The United States has played the dominant role—calling into question anxieties about declining American hegemony—and has successfully used a number of venues to press its concerns with developing country "free riders." These include support for greater participation of the less developed countries in GATT and tough conditionality on the part of the international financial institutions; regional initiatives that include deep integration components (NAFTA); bilateral negotiations, and unilateral threats.

Second, I have emphasized that the policy coordination must be understood as the outgrowth of political processes within the respective parties to the agreement. In the advanced industrial states, the push for the deeper integration of the developing countries has been driven by a wide array of interested parties, from particular industries such as financial services, to interest groups such as environmentalists. In the developing countries, the process of policy change pits reformist governments and new, more internationalist forces against those groups that have profited from the policy status quo.

The operation of these political factors makes it extremely difficult to calculate what the welfare consequences of any deep integration scheme are likely to be, for a given developing country or for the world as a whole. Three possibilities can be distinguished. First, developing countries through some combination of political and economic processes may unilaterally gravitate toward welfare-enhancing deep integration schemes. Second, developing country governments

---

1. Kahler (1993, p. 23).

may adopt deep integration measures under threat of external sanction, overriding domestic opponents or substantive reservations, but the policy change is nonetheless welfare improving. Countries are, in effect, pressured into realizing their own best interests (or at least the interests of some groups). However, a third possibility must be recognized: that external pressures reflect the interests of particular groups in the advanced industrial states or stem from analytically flawed models, and that deep integration schemes are therefore welfare reducing.

This perspective on the politics of deep integration raises three issues of significance to policymaking. The first concerns the organizational form that further initiatives for deep integration might take, especially the relative merits for the developing countries of multilateral versus regional organization.[2] The expanding nature of the deep integration agenda poses a second challenge to the developing countries. The third and most important question is whether the reform movement that has swept the developing world is politically sustainable.

Multilateralism or Regionalism?

One of the major debates about the organization of the world economy centers on the compatibility of multilateral and regional forms of international organization. As the regional studies have shown, this debate is clearly germane to developing countries, since two regions in which there has been much organizational innovation—Asia and the Western Hemisphere—have substantial numbers of important developing countries. Europe's regionalism is clearly less inclusive, but as discussed in chapter 5, developments in the European Union have implications not only for prospective members such as Turkey and the Eastern European countries, but also for the Mediterranean associates and the states of Africa, the Caribbean, and the Pacific.

The debate centers on whether regionalism is inherently discriminatory or whether it can remain "open" and provide the basis for

2. See Lawrence (forthcoming); Bhagwati (1993).

deeper multilateral integration.[3] Several points I have discussed are relevant to this controversy. The first is the growing interest of the developing countries in multilateralism; indeed, they are becoming one of its most important bases of support. The developing countries' views of GATT and the World Trade Organization (WTO) vary, but for several reasons a shift toward support has clearly taken place.

As policy reforms take root and are consolidated, they contribute to the emergence of new, internationalist groups tied to exports and foreign investment. As trade grows, and the trade policies of the advanced industrial states become more erratic, the advanced developing countries have come to see GATT and the new WTO as offering "protection against protection."[4] Even a well-institutionalized, rule-based regime with clear mechanisms for dispute settlement will not completely restrain powerful actors from behaving opportunistically. Nonetheless, the developing countries have a strong interest in increasing discipline over "gray area" measures and in institutionalizing stronger mechanisms for dispute settlement. The price to be paid for securing these benefits from the multilateral system is an acceptance of the expanded policy agenda of the advanced industrial states, and of the United States in particular. Therefore the WTO will probably become a more important locus for developing countries' negotiations on deep integration issues.

The nature of the economic reforms undertaken by the developing countries and the geographic structure of their trade and investment ties also affect the attitudes of the developing countries toward multilateralism. The interest in deeper integration has grown out of a broader drive for policy reform that is usually undertaken on an unconditional most favored nation basis. With the partial exception of Mexico, liberalization has not been linked to preferential arrangements, and even in Mexico, trade and investment reforms have generally been extended to all parties on a most favored nation basis.[5] Moreover, the trade and investment relations of most of the advanced developing countries are becoming more geographically diversified,

3. For accounts that see regionalism as largely benign, see Oye (1992, chap. 7); Lawrence (1992); Schott (1991); Aho and Ostry (1990); Bhagwati (1993); Haggard (1994). For a formal model of why regionalism might become discriminatory, see Krugman (1991).

4. My thanks to Van Whiting for bringing this phrase to my attention.

5. The exception, of course, is the rules of origin.

cutting across traditional definitions of region rather than being contained within them. As a result, multilateralism is likely to become an efficient and rational framework for the conduct of commercial diplomacy.

What, then, are the interests of the developing countries in regionalism? The regional arrangements discussed in chapters 3, 4, and 5 suggest that historical connections, propinquity, and the geographical structure of trade remain important. Mexico is more dependent on the American market than any other developing country that is a U.S. trading partner. It is thus not surprising that the two countries would seek a regional arrangement and that such an arrangement would go beyond what had been accomplished at the multilateral level to encompass matters of deep integration.

Given the welter of current proposals, the explosion of regional arrangements among the developing countries, and the dire predictions that competing regional blocs are developing, it is important to underline how little formal regionalization has actually taken place between North and South. To date, regional integration has not served as the main organizational vehicle for the deeper integration of the developing countries. Moreover, the regional route to deeper integration will probably not be as central as is sometimes thought.

The accession of Greece, Portugal, and Spain into the EC is a significant exception to the rule. Yet the circumstances surrounding their accession were unusual in several ways, not least in the existence of a well-formed institutional infrastructure and the willingness of the EC to extend substantial transfers to smooth the integration process. This offer was clearly not an open one, and it is highly unlikely that any of the emerging regional arrangements will offer similar cushioning mechanisms to developing country entrants. NAFTA is revealing; despite the extensive policy adjustments undertaken by Mexico, the United States has extended virtually no direct financial assistance to the country.[6]

6. This observation should, however, be qualified. First, the United States did support a reconciliation between Mexico and the International Monetary Fund in the late 1980s, which paved the way for Brady plan debt relief. Second, periodic evidence shows that the United States and other developed countries have stood ready to provide Mexico with substantial balance of payments support in potential crises. See for example, Anthony DePalma, "Mexico's Trading Allies Play Financial Bodyguard," *New York Times,* September 12, 1994, p. D2, on a fund designed to carry Mexico through any problems associated with the presidential election and the American response to the crisis of December 1994.

The regional studies have suggested that some proposed—or feared—regional arrangements are not likely to develop. An East Asian bloc linking Japan to developing countries in the region is unlikely, and the future of a Western Hemisphere initiative remains highly uncertain because of politics in both North and South America. Outside of NAFTA, which is unlikely to expand rapidly, the Asia-Pacific Economic Cooperation forum is the most promising regional arrangement linking North and South, and its formal agenda remains modest.

Other "regional" agreements linking the advanced and developing countries fall into several categories. None is yet seriously relevant to an analysis of the deep integration agenda. In the first category are preference schemes in which the initiative is in the hands of the advanced industrial states; these include the Caribbean Basin Initiative, the Lomé Conventions, and the EU's associate agreements. Second are consultative forums such as the post-ministerial conference of the Association of Southeast Asian Nations and the EU's various dialogues. Finally, regional arrangements among developing countries have experienced a renaissance, especially in Latin America, but these arrangements have so far focused primarily on shallow integration.[7]

If the southern European cases are excluded, only one regional arrangement knits together developed and developing countries and is based on principles of reciprocity rather than the unilateral extension of preferential treatment by the advanced country partners. That is NAFTA. The lessons to be drawn from NAFTA for other developing countries about the political economy of deep regional integration schemes are sobering, however. The concessions made by Mexico to American demands were sweeping and revised up to the last minute in order to secure support from opportunistic American legislators. NAFTA makes clear that regionalism does not obviate the basic dilemma of multilateralism and may even accentuate it: developing countries may enjoy larger gains from deep regional integration than do their counterparts in the North, but to secure those advantages, the weaker party to the regional agreement will also make greater concessions and adjustments.

NAFTA also demonstrates a second point. Even with extensive concessions, the advanced industrial states are likely to face political

7. For an overview of these arrangements, see de la Torre and Kelly (1992).

difficulties of their own in negotiating deep integration arrangements with developing countries. NAFTA proved highly divisive, and its extension to other countries is likely to be much more gradual than the expansive rhetoric of the Enterprise for the Americas Initiative or the Miami summit would suggest. Current debates about the incorporation of the Eastern European countries into the EU (widening versus deepening), the continuing cat-and-mouse game with respect to Turkey's membership in the European Union, and the rapid demise of proposals for free trade agreements between the United States and a number of its East Asian trading partners are testimony to these difficulties.[8]

There are two sources of political difficulty that one finds in negotiating deep integration agreements linking developed and developing countries. First, if the regional agreement is to rest on a reciprocal foundation, the developed country partner will have to make at least some concessions in return for the developing country's consideration of the deep integration agenda. These concessions include reducing barriers in sectors that enjoyed protection; in NAFTA, these concessions came in textiles and apparel and certain agricultural products. Developing countries are also likely to demand greater discipline in the use of unfair trade laws and selective safeguards and to favor impartial and binding dispute settlement mechanisms. For obvious reasons, these concessions are politically difficult to make, though the accession of the southern European states into the EC and NAFTA demonstrated that they are not necessarily impossible.

The management of regulatory differences is another political difficulty in North-South negotiations. North-South integration schemes can become politically controversial in the more advanced partner if they appear to harmonize downward to laxer standards or are not comprehensive in coverage. The environmental politics of NAFTA provides an example. Early drafts of NAFTA took a narrow view of the grounds on which sanitary and phytosanitary standards were justified and seemed to open the door to a relaxation of American standards. As Stephen Mumme summarizes, "The potential downward harmonization of sanitary and phytosanitary regulations affecting pesticide use, industrial and commercial uses of hazardous and toxic

---

8. On the rise and decline of the idea of free trade areas in the Pacific, see Schott (1989).

substances, and other less toxic uses of biological and chemical agents, appeared to environmentalists to undo 20 years of U.S. regulatory progress."[9] Not only were environmentalists able to secure promises that American standards would not be relaxed, but they were able to force the construction of an elaborate monitoring machinery in the side agreements, which will have the practical effect of pressuring Mexico to upgrade its environmental standards; indeed, the very intent of the side agreement was to "regionalize" American environmental legislation.

These difficulties do not preclude deeper regional integration between North and South, but they do suggest why initiatives such as a Free Trade Area of the Americas or a deepening of the Asia-Pacific Economic Cooperation forum into a regional free trade area are likely to face difficulties in negotiation. Yet the limitations on the regional model of deep integration do not mean that the pressures on the developing countries are likely to abate. To the contrary, developing countries are now experiencing multilateral and bilateral pressures on a host of new issues.

Deep Integration, the New Trade Policy Agenda, and the New Conditionality

The review of regional experiences in this book reveals that the agenda for deeper integration with the developing countries has clustered in several broad areas that differ somewhat from those under consideration among the advanced industrial states.[10] First, the effort to persuade developing countries to forgo activist industrial policies has been managed through laws on subsidies and dumping; unfair trade laws have been the central mechanism for handling disputes over competition policy. The United States has been especially interested in getting developing countries to pay greater attention to the protection of intellectual property rights. In both areas, serious questions arise about whether deep integration constitutes a good for the developing countries.[11]

---

9. Mumme (1993, p. 207).

10. One of the most notable differences is the absence of discussion of macroeconomic coordination.

11. For example, there is great controversy over whether the East Asian NICs profited from an export-oriented industrial policy; even the World Bank (1993b) has now allowed for the possibility. There are also strong arguments to be made that developing countries can benefit—at least up to some threshold of development—by free riding on technological developments elsewhere through loose intellectual property protection.

To date, the third and most extensive cluster of policies has centered on improving the regulatory climate for foreign investors. Though typically considered a component of shallow integration, I argue that the liberalization of policies governing foreign investment and the granting of national treatment has typically been accompanied by broader regulatory changes designed to bring national policy into line with accepted international norms and practices. This interest has been pursued directly through negotiations on trade-related investment measures and the liberalization of "trade" in services, but also through encouragement of other reforms that have repercussions for foreign investors, including privatization, financial market deregulation, and reform of domestic competition policies and commercial law. In general, there seems to be a stronger analytic case that these reforms have been welfare improving, though they have clearly had great distributive consequences.

In the past five years, the range of "trade" issues has widened yet again. Environmental and labor standards constitute the most politically contentious issues to crowd their way onto the policy agenda, and the ones that are likely to be most relevant to developing countries. The scope of international environmental concerns is extremely wide and encompasses problems from transborder pollution (acid rain), to commons problems (global warming and ozone depletion), to issues of conservation and protection of endangered species. Yet trade and the environment have been linked most closely in discussions of the consequences of divergent environmental policies under conditions of free trade and investment.[12]

Environmentalists argue that the existence of differing standards gives industries the opportunity to migrate to pollution-friendly locations.[13] This in itself would not necessarily pose a problem were it not

12. I exclude from consideration the more sweeping argument that trade liberalization and an expansion of trade may be environmentally harmful in itself. The argument is typically made about the environmental consequences of unregulated commodity exports; timber is often cited as an example. See French (1993, pp. 9–23).

13. Such migration could occur through actual relocation by multinational firms or through the effects on comparative advantage associated with different environmental standards. See French (1993). Reviews of empirical studies by Low and Yeats (1992) and Carbaugh and Wassink (1992) find little empirical evidence for the migration hypothesis, though both admit the methodological difficulties involved. For overviews of the trade-environment link, see Charnovitz (1992, 1993); Thomas and Teroposky (1993).

for the fear of competitive deregulation or the "race to the bottom"; strong environmental legislation becomes politically more difficult if industry and labor believe that it will have adverse competitive consequences. The solution to this problem, it is argued, is regulatory harmonization. The contentious issue in the eyes of developing countries is over the nature of such harmonization and how to achieve it.

A watershed case in focusing debate was the 1991 dispute over an American embargo on the import of Mexican tuna. Under the American Marine Mammal Protection Act (MMPA) of 1972 and its subsequent amendments, Congress authorized the government to ban the import of commercial fish products that were caught with the aid of technology that resulted in much greater incidental mortality of marine mammals (particularly dolphins) than occurred in the United States. As Joel Trachtman notes, "Two concerns motivated Congress to link the import ban to compliance with U.S.-type regulatory standards: first, the protection of dolphins; second, the protection of the competitiveness of U.S. fishermen required to bear the regulatory costs imposed by the MMPA."[14] However, the National Marine Fisheries Service was slow in developing regulations to force foreign compliance with these standards, and in 1990 a California environmental group brought suits that led to the import ban.

Mexico demanded GATT consultations and finally called for a panel, arguing that the import ban violated the prohibition of quantitative restrictions, the prohibition on discriminatory application of such restrictions, and the requirement to accord national treatment.[15] The United States, by contrast, argued that the measures imposed were wholly internal regulations permitted under GATT article III. The panel found in Mexico's favor, in part by interpreting article III to permit the regulation of products but not the production processes used to make them. Nonetheless, Mexico dropped the case because of concerns about its possible effects on the negotiation of NAFTA.[16]

Though the panel finding on tuna and the signing of the side agreements were widely criticized by environmentalists and labor activists, their importance for the developing countries had less to do

14. See Trachtman (1992, p. 144); Black (1992).

15. The discriminatory element of the American law sprang from the fact that the ban was limited to imports from the Eastern Tropical Pacific.

16. In fact, President Salinas went further by announcing the implementation of a dolphin protection plan. See "Divine Porpoise," *Economist,* October 5, 1991, p. 31.

with the legal results than it did with the willingness of environmental and labor groups to seek to extend the scope of American regulation *and* to enforce that regulation unilaterally through an embargo. Steve Charnovitz has rightly argued that the line between multilateralism and unilateralism is more blurred than is often recognized, since multilateral agreements are ultimately enforced through sanctions. The Montreal Protocol is the oft-cited example; it mandates that members of the protocol are forbidden from importing chlorofluorocarbons from nonsignatories not complying with the phaseout provisions of the treaty.[17] However, the chief difference is that the Montreal Protocol is a multilateral agreement with more than one hundred signatories who found the sanctions provision in their interest. U.S. action to extend the standards of the MMPA, by contrast, reflected only American preferences.

The nature of the issues raised by the Mexican tuna case are parallel to the growing discussion of labor standards and workers' rights in the context of trade policy: in both cases, lax standards are seen as morally wrong and as providing unfair competitive advantages.[18] The International Labor Organization has overseen a proliferation of international labor standards, and the European Community has debated the issue of a communitywide social charter for two decades. But these efforts had little consequence for developing countries until they were linked with the possibility of enforcement through trade sanctions.

Again, the United States has been the leader, though it is quite possible to imagine future alliances on this issue with the European social democracies.[19] Beginning in 1984, eligibility for U.S. trade preferences under the Generalized System of Preferences was made conditional on an acceptable standard for workers' rights, and in 1988, the Trade and Competitiveness Act stipulated that failure to provide certain workers' rights could be considered an "unreasonable" trade practice against which the United States could retaliate under section 301. Though the powers under the 1988 bill were never deployed the United States did periodically remove GSP privileges. It was, however, NAFTA that focused attention on the issue and pro-

17. Charnovitz (1993, p. 156).
18. See Herzenberg and Perez-Lopez (1990); Charnovitz (1992).
19. For a review of U.S. policy see Herzenberg and Perez-Lopez (1990); Amato (1990).

vided an opening for organized labor to regain some of the voice that it has lost on trade questions; the result was the creation of the oversight machinery outlined in appendix C. Though the use of this machinery had not been tested at the time of this writing, American labor organizations had clearly signaled their intent to use the NAFTA process to press tougher labor standards on Mexico.[20]

Very little empirical work has been done on the effect of different labor standards on labor market conditions, productivity, competitiveness, or growth.[21] Much will clearly depend on the stringency of the standard, its effect on a nation's economy, and how it is enforced. At the extreme are standards such as the demand for wage convergence through increasing minimum wages or even tying wage growth to productivity growth, which could amount to little more than a denial of the principle of comparative advantage. These moves can only be viewed as purely protectionist and thus welfare reducing. At the other extreme are standards such as freedom from forced labor that have an important humanitarian rationale but are unlikely to greatly affect the overall competitiveness of even the most repressive countries.

The enforcement mechanism has welfare consequences too. If sanctions are employed, or even if they are threatened to enforce a standard that does not respond to a clear market failure, then it will have welfare-reducing consequences for both parties. Positive inducements, however, such as technical assistance to labor organizations in the low-wage country or an expansion of trade adjustment assistance in the high-wage country could be welfare improving. Nonetheless, it is important to stress not only that very little is known about the probable effects of imposing labor standards, but that public policy on labor issues is vulnerable to political processes in both the developed or the developing countries that will not necessarily yield an optimal result.

Debates about the link between trade and environmental and labor standards issues are mirrored closely in recent discussions of conditionality (see chapter 2).[22] With the end of the cold war, international

20. See Allen R. Myerson, "Big Labor's Strategic Raid in Mexico," *New York Times*, September 12, 1994, p. D1.

21. A valuable theoretical introduction to the issues is provided by Brown, Deardorff, and Stern (1993).

22. An excellent introduction to the issues is provided in a series of publications from the Overseas Development Council. See Nelson and Eglington (1992) on promot-

donors began to revise their aid programs to reflect the declining significance of geostrategic concerns and the increasing salience of other goals, including environmental protection, poverty reduction, and reduced military spending. One feature of the new conditionality is the addition of conditions that are explicitly political, including human rights, participatory development, improved governance, and even democracy.

As in the case of trade linkages, the new conditionality reveals mixed motives and a questionable analytic underpinning. On the one hand, the new conditionality responds to noble normative concerns, yet it is also assumed optimistically that "all good things go together." For example, it is assumed that political changes, such as democratization, are good for development and that political conditionality will improve the prospects that democracy will flourish. However, most of the evidence in the political science literature is skeptical about both claims; democracy appears unrelated to economic performance, and there is little evidence that conditionality is likely to affect democracy's prospects.[23] Another source of skepticism comes from the burdens such conditionality places on donors and recipient governments and the growing inconsistency among competing goals as the list of conditions is lengthened.

As with the use of trade sanctions to enforce standards, the welfare consequences of the new conditionality will depend not only on the substance of the policy reform being sought, but on the mechanism of enforcement. For example, what Joan Nelson and Stephanie Eglington call "allocative conditionality" has a reward and a punishment component: donors provide more aid to countries that meet certain criteria, a positive inducement, but take aid away from those that do not. Aggregate welfare could conceivably be reduced if the loss in aid is greater than the gains from the policy reform. Despite appearances, this brief book is not designed as a critique of deeper integration; there is little doubt that many of the reforms undertaken by the developing countries in the past decade, including several deep inte-

---

ing democracy; Nelson and Eglington (1993) on multiple conditionality; Lewis (1992) on conditionality in favor of the poor; and Ball (1992) on conditionality aimed at reducing military expenditure.

23. For a representative review of the relationship between democracy and growth, see Przeworski and Limongi (1993). On the influence of conditionality on democracy, see Nelson and Eglington (1992, 1993).

gration measures, have been salutary. However, our understanding of the effects of the welfare consequences of shallow integration measures is much greater than our understanding of deep integration measures, and on those grounds alone there is good reason to remain agnostic and cautious. As Miles Kahler has noted, there even seems to be a trend away from deep integration through harmonization; the European Community, for example, has increasingly opted for a model of mutual recognition that accepts national differences.[24]

When domestic politics in the advanced industrial states, particularly in the United States, is considered, the case for agnosticism is strengthened. When policy convergence is achieved through the exercise of leverage, the greatest cited benefit is often that reaching agreement precluded an even more restrictive outcome. This is faint praise indeed. In such situations, it may be better to refrain from opening the Pandora's box of negotiations rather than suffer the consequences that such negotiations might bring; as I suggested in chapter 3, this impulse appears to be at least part of the motivation behind Asian resistance to a deepening of the Asia-Pacific Economic Cooperation forum.

The Domestic Politics of Deep Integration

The economic policy changes in the developing world in the past ten years have been profound, and there are reasonable grounds to believe that they will yield fruit and become politically consolidated. As they do, it is also reasonable to believe that the developing countries will gravitate toward at least some components of the deep integration agenda. That threshold has not yet been crossed in all countries, however, especially in those where the reform experience is more recent, such as in Latin America and Africa. Certain domestic political factors in the developing world are likely to determine the pace of deeper integration with the world economy.

In their response to the crises of the 1980s, governments came up with reform packages that centered primarily on macroeconomic policy and other measures that were administratively easy and could be taken with the stroke of a pen; trade reform is an example.

24. Kahler (1993).

However, the next stage of reforms—and the policy changes required by deep integration—typically involve institutional changes that are more time-consuming and less well understood, such as building regulatory and enforcement capacity.[25] Intellectual property rights provides a clear example; much of the current controversy between the United States and the developing countries on this issue centers not on the laws themselves but on the judicial system and enforcement mechanisms. In such settings, even committed governments may face difficulties in complying with international commitments.

Another more profound issue concerns the political sustainability of reforms. I have just emphasized the uncertainties about the social welfare consequences of reform. Yet for politics, these aggregate effects—still frequently uncertain—are less significant than the distributive consequences of the reforms. The implicit political economy of reform that undergirds calls for deeper integration rests on the assumption that if such reforms are undertaken, new constituencies of beneficiaries will emerge that will counterbalance resistance from those who are temporary losers. Yet this assumption is far from assured, and the political success of such reforms will in the end hinge on factors beyond the scope of this book, including the institutions of government, the development of stable party systems, and the strategy and tactics of compensation.[26]

Finally, there is an intangible political factor that is frequently treated as an atavistic residue destined to fade with time; this is nationalist resistance to deeper integration with the world economy. The profound failures of nationalist development policies are well known. But the political problems of deep integration through leverage, as well as the existence of successful nationalist strategies, such as those in the East Asian newly industrializing countries, suggest that caution about deeper integration may have a rational foundation in some cases.

---

25. See Haggard and Kaufman (1992); Naim (1994).

26. See Haggard and Kaufman (1992); Bates and Krueger (1993); Williamson (1993); Haggard and Webb (1994).

Comments

Sebastian Edwards

The 1990s have been years of increasing economic integration throughout the world. Scores of countries have liberalized their trade accounts, reducing import tariffs and eliminating quantitative restrictions. Remarkably, after years of hesitation, a large number of developing nations have joined the more advanced countries in implementing trade liberalization reforms. For example, most of the Latin American nations, which since the 1930s had favored an import substitution development strategy, went through gigantic unilateral trade reforms in the late 1980s and early 1990s. Moreover, the Latin American countries are now eagerly pursuing free trade agreements with the United States, something almost unthinkable only a few years ago. Similar trade liberalization processes are taking place in Asia, where countries that for decades had pursued highly protectionist policies—India is the most startling example—are implementing major efforts aimed at dismantling trade barriers. There is little doubt that, as the end of the century approaches, the view that freer trade and liberalization is conducive to improved economic performance has become the dominant one in academic as well as policy circles. The proponents of more open commercial policies have decisively won the decades-old debate between *outward orientation* and *inward*

Sebastian Edwards is Henry Ford II Professor of Economics at the Anderson Graduate School of Management, University of California, Los Angeles; and chief economist, Latin America and the Caribbean, World Bank.

He is grateful to Fernando Losada for his assistance in the preparation of these comments.

123

orientation. The approval of GATT's Uruguay Round in December 1993 has added impetus to the global efforts to open international trade.

This process has generated a number of fundamental questions: What has been the role of external forces—including the multilateral organizations—in the developing nations' move toward integrationist policies? Are these reform processes politically consolidated or, as the political upheaval in Mexico seems to suggest, are they still somewhat weak? Will these processes, which until now have been mostly restricted to opening up international trade, broaden in scope? More specifically, will *deep integration* policies be pursued by the developing nations in the short run?

Stephan Haggard has tackled many of these questions in his useful book. His treatment of the U.S. diplomatic-cum-economic pressures to persuade developing countries to open up to international competition is particularly interesting. In this comment I expand on some of Haggard's points, by taking a broader perspective. Instead of insisting, as he does, on taking an almost exclusive U.S.-centered view, I make an effort to approach these issues from the developing countries' perspective. As a result I take some issue with Haggard's interpretation of the role of the United States and the multilateral institutions—the International Monetary Fund and the World Bank, in particular—in the adoption of liberalization policies in the developing nations, and especially in Latin America. I first discuss the causes behind the liberalization policies in Latin America, arguing that these policies were the result of a complex interaction of factors and not simply the imposition of a blueprint from the so-called Washington consensus. Second, I deal with the liberalization of capital movements. I evaluate some of the most important economic arguments used to delay the opening up of the capital account in many countries, and in particular in Asia. In dealing with this issue I draw on some of the lessons of the recent (December 1994) Mexican crisis.[1]

Openness and the New Development Paradigm in Latin America

Why did the Latin American countries, which for decades had pursued inward-looking and protectionist development strategies,

---

1. Haggard deals with the first issue in his chapters 2 and 4; he addresses the second question in his chapters 1 and 3.

begin to open their economies to international competition in the late 1980s and early 1990s? Stephan Haggard deals with this issue in chapters 1, 2, and 4 of this book and concludes that this shift in policy orientation was largely the result of both internal circumstances and changing *external* conditions. According to him the four fundamental external forces behind this policy shift were the international debt crisis of 1982; the policies of the international financial institutions, which in the aftermath of the crisis conditioned their loans to policy changes; pressures by the industrial countries through retaliatory commercial policies; and the changes in the regime governing international trade. In chapter 4 on Latin America Haggard analyzes how these factors have affected the opening of economies in the region, in particular Brazil and Mexico. Analyzing the relative importance of external and internal forces in the development of Latin America's policy shift goes beyond mere doctrinaire debates. It can shed important light on the issue of the sustainability of the reforms. A policy stance largely imposed from abroad has a very small chance of becoming permanent; however, new ideas that respond to the region's internal dynamics are more likely to have a lasting effect.

Although it is not possible to deny that external factors, especially the multilateral institutions, had a role in the forging of the new Latin American views, in my opinion it is an exaggeration to give them central billing in this process. An interpretation closer to history would give a fundamental role to the soul searching that began in Latin America in the early 1980s. The three most important elements in this process were the failure of the heterodox programs implemented in the mid-1980s in Argentina, Brazil, and Peru—the Austral, Cruzado, and APRA plans—the example of the East Asian countries with outward-oriented policies, especially the contrasting experiences of these countries and the Latin American nations; and the reinterpretation of the Chilean experience with market orientation since the mid-1970s. Although the role of the multilateral institutions was less central than has sometimes been argued, they did exercise some influence in forging the new convergence of doctrinal views in Latin America. These institutions influenced policy positions in Latin America through several channels, including empirical research, economic and sector analytical work, lending practices, policy dialogue, and conditionality. In this section of my comments I deal in some detail with the influence of events in East Asia, or more accurately, with Latin America's interpretation of East Asia's experience in Latin America. I also discuss the Chilean reforms.[2]

The East Asian Experience

For decades most economists in Latin America basically ignored the developments in East Asia. All interest in comparative economics was centered on Europe and the socialist countries.[3] However, in the mid- to late-1980s, and as a result of the debt crisis a series of comparative studies, including some early ones sponsored by the UN Economic Commission for Latin America (CEPAL), contrasted the experiences of the Latin nations with those of East Asia, with the objective of trying to understand why economic performance, and especially growth, had been stronger in the latter. These analyses highlighted four fundamental policy differences among these two groups of countries. First, East Asia had avoided excessive and variable protectionist policies. Second, and perhaps more important, since the mid-1960s the East Asian nations had stayed away from overvalued exchange rates and real exchange rate volatility. Third, contrary to the Latin American countries, the East Asian nations maintained a stable macroeconomic environment, high saving rates, and low and steady rates of inflation. And fourth, the East Asian nations had significantly fewer, and simpler, regulations. [4]

Although between 1965 and 1980 the two groups of countries had similar rates of growth—Latin America with a 6 percent average and East Asia with 7 percent—their export performance was very different. While real exports grew at an annual average of 10 percent in East Asia, they *declined* at a pace of 1 percent a year in Latin America and the Caribbean. Moreover, while income inequality was reduced in East Asia, it increased in Latin America during this period.

The marked difference in export behavior across the two regions was possibly what impressed Latin American leaders the most. In

2. Edwards (1995) contains a full discussion of the failed heterodox stabilization efforts in Latin America during the "muddling through" (1982–87) period.

3. An analysis of Latin America's most prestigious economics journal *El Trimestre Económico* reveals that between 1960 and 1980 not one article dealing with the East Asian experiences was published.

4. See Lin (1988); Balassa (1988); Bianchi and Nohara (1988); World Bank (1993b).

particular, the rapid export expansion in Korea since the 1960s—a country that during the 1950s had not performed significantly differently than the Latin American nations—became a source of keen interest. Chin-Yuan Lin reports that between 1949 and 1960 real export earnings grew at a lower rate in South Korea (3.9 percent a year) than in Chile (4.3 percent).[5] During that period real GDP grew in South Korea at the rather modest rate of 3.8 percent a year, not much different from Argentina's average of 3.6 percent. However, starting in the mid-1960s things changed dramatically in Korea: between 1963 and 1990 Korea's merchandise exports grew, in *real* U.S. dollar terms, at an annual rate of 23 percent. This stellar performance has often been mentioned as a premier example of the positive results of outward-oriented policies.[6]

However, as Haggard points out, Korea has not always been an open economy. In fact, throughout most of 1950–63 Korea's external sector was highly distorted. Import substitution policies were followed with great zeal during this period: most imports were subject to licensing, tariff rates were high (exceeding 50 percent in 1959–60), and a multiple exchange rate system was in effect.[7] With the exception of 1961–62, the National Bureau of Economic Research project on trade regimes classified Korea as a "highly repressed" economy throughout these years.[8] A major policy change took place in 1964, when exchange rates were unified, a major devaluation was implemented, and a systematic process of outward orientation was started. At the same time the accumulation of human capital, through an improvement in the coverage and quality of education, was encouraged, and basic infrastructure projects were pursued. Gradually, import tariffs were reduced, the coverage of import licenses was eased, and import prohibitions were eliminated. At the same time massive programs aimed at encouraging exports were implemented. By the end of the 1980s, Korea's average import tariffs had been reduced to approximately 10 percent, and import licenses had been virtually eliminated.[9] The transformation of Korea's external sector not only resulted in an accelerated growth of exports, but also affected their composition.

5. Lin (1988).
6. Krueger (1990).
7. Balassa (1988).
8. Bhagwati (1978); Krueger (1978).
9. Edwards (1993).

Though in 1962 manufactured goods amounted to a mere 17 percent of total exports, by 1980 their share had climbed to 75 percent.[10]

Supporting exchange rate and export promotion policies accompanied the Korean trade liberalization experience throughout 1964–93. Since the devaluation of 1964, the Korean authorities have made a concerted effort to maintain a highly depreciated—that is, competitive—*real* exchange rate. This contrasted sharply with the Latin American countries, where historically exchange rate overvaluation was a norm, and real exchange rate volatility was rampant.[11]

Starting in the 1960s an aggressive export promotion scheme became an important complement of the Korean trade liberalization strategy. Throughout the years exports have been subsidized through a number of channels, including (a) direct cash subsidies (until 1964); (b) direct tax reductions (until 1973); (c) interest rate preferences; (d) indirect tax reductions on intermediate inputs; and (e) tariff exemptions to imported intermediate materials.[12] Kwang Kim has recently calculated that these subsidies were reduced from 23 percent to zero between 1963 and 1983. He has argued, as others have, that in Korea, export subsidies were important during the earlier years of the Korean export boom.[13]

A recent massive study undertaken by the World Bank has explored in great detail the causes behind the East Asian export success.[14] It is argued that in most cases the government organized "contests" among private firms, with export performance as the main criterion to determine "winners." Those firms with a strong export record were rewarded with access to preferential credit and other types of special treatment. According to this study the most important element of East Asia's success was that the export-promotion policies were strictly result oriented. If a scheme did not generate results in the form of higher exports in a relatively short period of time, it was promptly canceled. More important, this study has argued that the implementation of selective industrial policies that introduced distortions within the export sector, did *not* play an important role in East Asia's

10. Kim (1991).
11. See Arellano (1989) for a comparison of exchange rate policy in Latin America and East Asia. See also Edwards (1989).
12. See Kim (1991) for details on the different export promotion schemes used.
13. In Latin America, there has been a controversy on the actual effectiveness of export subsidies. See, for example, Nogues and Gulati (1992).
14. World Bank (1993b).

success story. The study reached this conclusion on the basis of three related pieces of evidence. First, the authors found that, when compared with an international benchmark, those sectors that were heavily promoted—for instance, chemicals and basic metals in Korea—were not bigger than those labor-intensive sectors that were not promoted by the authorities. Second, the study found that total factor productivity growth was not faster in promoted than in non-promoted sectors.[15] And third, the study argues that the failure of Korea's effort to develop a heavy and chemical industry in the 1980s provides prima facie evidence of the lack of success of selective policies.

Ching-Yuan Lin has compared in some detail trade policies in Korea, Taiwan, and Argentina.[16] His computations indicate that in the 1970s the overall rate of effective protection was 10 percent in South Korea, 5 percent in Taiwan, and 47 percent in Argentina. The contrast was even bigger in the manufacturing sector, where the effective rates of protection were –1 percent in Korea, 19 percent in Taiwan, and almost 100 percent in Argentina. These differences in protective rates affected relative incentives, generating a substantial anti-export bias in Argentina. Modern theories of economic growth have linked openness with productivity growth: more open economies tend to engage in technological innovation faster, exhibiting more rapid productivity improvements. According to Lin labor productivity increased 8.7 percent annually in Korea during 1973–85, and only 0.5 percent annually in Argentina. The vigorous growth experienced by other East Asian countries—including the second-generation "miracle" countries, Malaysia, Thailand, and Indonesia—since the late 1980s has added impetus to the idea that a development path based on openness and market orientation can be extremely rewarding. Increasingly, Latin American leaders are turning toward East Asia for inspiration and economic partnership.

The conduct of macroeconomic policy constitutes a second crucial difference between East Asia and Latin America. Inflation has been significantly higher in the Latin American nations than in the East Asian countries. Moreover, Latin America has also been affected by higher inflation variability and real exchange rate volatility. The great-

15. World Bank (1993b, pp. 312–13, 316).
16. Lin (1988).

est advantage of a stable macroeconomic environment is that it reduces uncertainty, encouraging savings and, thus, allowing a higher
rate of investment. To the extent that the real exchange rate is stable,
investment in the tradables sector will increase, as will exports.

In a series of papers Jeffrey Sachs has hypothesized that politics and
income distribution play an important role in explaining the differences in macroeconomic policies in Latin America and East Asia.[17] In
particular, Sachs argues that exchange rate management, and especially devaluations, have had very different political consequences in
the two regions. While in East Asia real exchange rate overvaluation
(and delayed corrective measures) negatively affected a relatively
large number of tradable goods producers in the rural sector, in Latin
America it only affected a relatively small number of large (and many
times absentee) landowners (*latifundistas*). Thus, while in East Asia
macroeconomic mismanagement had high political costs by offend-
ing many small landowners, in Latin America it had relatively little
political consequence. In fact, by allowing artificially low prices on
food and other tradables, real exchange rate overvaluation in Latin
America has traditionally benefited the politically powerful urban
working class.

The increased interest among some senior CEPAL staff members
in exploring differences between East Asia and Latin America during
the mid- and late-1980s played an important role in the development
of the new consensus. In another study I have argued that in a way
this development was like "Nixon in China."[18] When the one institution that had for decades defended inward orientation expressed
doubts about the policy and recognized that lessons could be learned
from East Asia's experience with outward-oriented policies, it was
difficult to dismiss the evaluation as purely "neoliberal" propaganda.
In that regard, the joint project between CEPAL and the Institute of
Developing Economies in Tokyo on the comparative experiences of
the two regions, undertaken during 1987, was a pivotal event.[19] Also,
a major study, conducted during that same year by Fernando Fajnzylber—one of CEPAL's most respected theoreticians—and later
published, was highly influential in pointing out the differences in

---

17. Sachs (1987, 1989).
18. Edwards (1995).
19. The results from this study were published as Bianchi and Nohara (1988).

performance in the two regions and the need for major changes in the direction of Latin America's economic policies.[20] This document later became the core of the innovative, and "convergent," CEPAL blueprint for the 1990s that emphasizes the need for combining market-oriented structural reforms with targeted policies toward the poor.[21]

The "discovery" of East Asia, and in particular the contrasting experiences of those countries and Latin America, has resulted in deliberate attempts to learn more about these experiences and emulate the policies. The World Bank's *East Asia Miracle* has become a bestseller among policymakers, politicians, and academics throughout Latin America; seminars on East Asia are increasingly common and a number of countries in the region have expressed their desire to join the Asia-Pacific Economic Cooperation forum—Chile and Mexico are already members.

Market Orientation in Chile and the Opening of Latin America

Chile initiated its market-oriented reforms in 1974, almost a decade before the other Latin American countries. Initially the Chilean experience was looked at with skepticism and mistrust. Many analysts argued that the Chilean reforms were exotic and could only be undertaken by an authoritarian regime. In the late 1980s and early 1990s, however, as the Chilean economy recovered with great vigor, political leaders throughout Latin America began to look closely at this experience in an effort to gain insights and inspiration. The Chilean experiment gained greatly in stature as a role model once it became apparent that the new democratic government of President Patricio Aylwin had embraced, and furthered, some of the main elements of the market reforms first implemented during the military regime.

During the 1970s and early 1980s the Chilean approach to reform was severely criticized inside Chile; prominent economists grouped in the opposition think tank CIEPLAN launched a series

20. Fajnzylber (1990).

21. CEPAL (1992). Although the change in views in CEPAL is evident to any careful reader of its documents, it is important to recognize that there are still some important differences of opinion within that institution.

of attacks against the program.[22] It was mainly criticized on three accounts: its excessive reliance on free prices and market forces; the reduced role of the government in economic matters; and the opening of international trade and financial transactions to foreign competition.

The opening of the Chilean economy, which resulted in the *unilateral*—without any pressure from the United States or major inducement from the World Bank or IMF—reduction of import tariffs to a uniform level of 10 percent, gave rise to the most abundant attacks. Critics argued that Chile should abandon the experiment and move rapidly toward a program in which the state would play a central role in supporting key industries through higher tariffs and other forms of subsidies. For instance, in a 1983 collection published by CIEPLAN it was argued by Alejandro Foxley that "the State should articulate a 'vision' about the country's productive future. . . . The idea is to pick and develop 'winners' . . . . [To this effect] the State would use every instrument available. . . , including special credit lines, subsidies, import tariffs and tax exemptions."[23]

Starting in 1985 the Chilean economy began to recover vigorously. And, by 1989, it had accumulated a very strong record of growth, which surprised most analysts including the domestic critics. As the presidential elections of 1989 approached, it had become clear that the criticism of a market-based development path had greatly subsided. In fact, the three presidential candidates presented remarkably similar economic proposals that shared many of the important elements. Most important, future president Patricio Aylwin's program—drafted mostly by the CIEPLAN group—expressed a substantial sense of continuity in regard to the most important market-oriented policies. The program argued for "low import tariffs," and for ensuring that the economy had "positive real interest rates that maintain

22. See, for example, Arellano (1982); Cortazar (1982); Foxley (1982, 1983a, 1983b); Meller (1984). During the Pinochet regime the military did not allow open political discussions. As a result, debates on economic policy became a substitute for political discussions. The CIEPLAN economists played an important (and brave) role in maintaining some sense of perspective in Chile during these years.

23. See Foxley (1983b, pp. 42–44). He suggests that under democratic rule import tariffs should be increased to an average of 30 percent, with a maximum effective rate of protection of 60 percent. He argued, however, that these policies would "not result in a return to the import substitution model, as was known in Chile and Latin America during the 1950s and 1960s" (p. 54).

some relation with productivity."[24] By early 1990 it was clear to perceptive analysts that the incoming government was not going to fiddle with the main elements of the market reforms. If anything, the new authorities were soon ready to move even further in some areas, such as the opening of the economy and the reduction of import tariffs.[25] In fact, an early and highly significant decision undertaken by the incoming administration was to slash import tariffs by one-third.[26]

The Aylwin government's decision to maintain the main aspects of the market reforms was clearly stated by the recently appointed minister of finance, Alejandro Foxley, in a 1990 interview: "Preserving the former government achievements means maintaining an open economy fully integrated into world markets, dynamic growth in exports, with a private sector fully committed to the task of [economic] development.[27]

Although once in power the leaders of the new democratic Chilean government firmly supported some of the most fundamental market reforms of the 1970s and 1980s, they still had some important disagreements with the former rulers regarding the role of social-oriented and redistributive policies. In that regard Foxley was equally clear in the 1990 interview: "Remedying the former government shortcomings means recapturing the balance between economic growth and the deteriorated conditions of the middle and, above all, the lower classes."

What is especially important, however, is that in seeking funding for new social programs the new Chilean government strongly and decisively rejected traditional formulas based on inflationary finance. Quite the contrary, the new administration made it clear from day one that the only way of increasing social spending without generating unsustainable macroeconomic pressures was by finding solid sources

24. See Edwards and Edwards (1991) for a discussion of the Aylwin program.

25. The Aylwin government reduced import tariffs to a uniform 11 percent and declined participating in new regional integration efforts for fear that they would be "too protectionist."

26. Tariffs were reduced to 11 percent across the board in June of 1991. The newly appointed independent Central Bank played an important role in further opening the economy during this period. In a very incisive article, Fontaine (1992) has argued that by 1989 the majority of Chilean voters were still skeptical about the merits of the market-oriented reforms. According to him the process of convergence and synthesis began with the intellectual elites of the Socialist and Christian Democrat parties.

27. *Newsweek* (Latin American edition), March 26, 1990.

of government revenues. Additionally, the new government continued the policy of focusing social programs on the poor and avoiding the blanket subsidies that had historically benefited the middle and upper classes. In short, the populist policies of yesteryear had no role in the new Chilean government.

An important political decision made by the new government was to address head on, and during the first year of the administration, two critical economic reforms: a tax package aimed at funding the new social programs, and a reform of the labor law that had been criticized by unions leaders and some political commentators. Government officials were careful to explain that these two pieces of legislation constituted the *only* important changes to the economic model of Pinochet. In this way, and especially by tackling these issues early on, the government sought to minimize possible negative effects on private investment associated with policy uncertainty. This strategy is clearly discussed in a perceptive document by Minister of the Presidency Edgardo Boeninger: "The administration first undertook the task of implementing reforms producing either uncertainty or cost increases in the economy (tax reform and changes in labor legislation). These have now [March 1991] been mostly completed, enabling the government to guarantee full stability of the rules of the economic game for the rest of its term, thus facilitating dynamic behavior by business."[28]

Today, in the midst of the Mexican peso crisis, Chile stands alone as the most successful "early reformer." Its example, including the policies followed at the macro and micro level, guides policymakers in many of the Latin American countries contemplating, or pursuing, policies aimed at integrating their economies with those of the rest of the world. Interestingly enough, Chile remains hesitant about a number of items on the "deep integration" agenda. In particular, as I argue in the following pages, Chile has been very reluctant to relax capital controls.

Capital Controls and Deep Integration

As Haggard points out in chapter 1, one of the fundamental features of deep integration is extending the opening process beyond

28. Boeninger (1991).

goods and services, toward the free mobility of factors, especially capital. However, as is amply documented by Haggard, although impediments to international trade in goods and (to some extent) services have been greatly reduced, restrictions on capital movements are widespread, especially among the newly industrialized and developing nations. In this section of my comments I evaluate some of the most important arguments made by policymakers in (many) developing countries to oppose, or delay, the relaxation of capital controls and the opening of the capital account. I argue that the debacle of fixed parities within the European Monetary System in 1992 and 1993, as well as the Mexican peso crisis of December 1994 have strengthened many of these arguments. Moreover, I believe that the Mexican crisis has effectively provided a temporary blow to the forces of deep integration in the developing nations.

During the past decade or so advanced and poorer countries have dealt with capital movements very differently. Restrictions to capital mobility have been greatly reduced in the most advanced nations, especially in the European Community since 1992. It has been estimated that, largely as a result of the relaxation of capital restrictions in the industrial countries, the turnover in foreign exchange markets more than tripled between 1986 and 1993, with total (net) daily turnover exceeding U.S.$1,000 billion. As Lars Svensson has pointed out, this figure is remarkably high when compared with the total *stock* of reserves held by the industrial countries' central banks—in the spring of 1992 the G-10 held approximately U.S.$400 billion in official reserves.[29] In stark contrast to the liberalization process in the advanced countries, capital controls and impediments continue to be pervasive among the developing nations. Manuel Guitián has pointed out that the multilateral institutions have traditionally considered restrictions on trade on goods to be significantly more harmful than impediments to capital mobility.[30] For example, while the Articles of Agreement of the International Monetary Fund condemn the use of trade restrictions, they condone the use of capital controls.[31] Moreover, during the past few years most multilateral negotiations to reduce barriers on international exchange—including GATT's Uru-

29. Svensson (1993).
30. Guitián (forthcoming).
31. Article 6, section 3.

guay Round—have concentrated on trade on goods and services, virtually ignoring capital controls.

As documented by Haggard the United States has recently urged a number of developing nations—especially the East Asian countries—to relax capital controls and to open their capital accounts.[32] However, this proposition has been met with skepticism and, in some cases, resistance. The apprehension regarding the opening of the capital account—or at least its rapid opening—goes beyond traditional nationalistic views and is based on both macro- and micro-economic arguments. It is often argued that under full capital mobility the national authorities lose (some) control over monetary policy, and that the economy will become more vulnerable to external shocks. Also, policymakers have often expressed concerns over their (effective) freedom for selecting the exchange rate regime if capital is highly mobile. Moreover, sometimes it has been argued that full capital mobility will result in "overborrowing" and, eventually, in a major debt crisis as occurred in Latin America in 1982 or in the more recent currency crisis in Mexico. Other concerns about the liberalization of capital movements relate to increased real exchange rate instability and loss of international competitiveness. Still other analysts have pointed out that the premature opening of the capital account could lead to massive capital flight from the country in question. This type of discussion has led to a growing literature on the most adequate sequencing and speed of liberalization and stabilization reforms.[33]

An important problem that has been addressed when designing a liberalization strategy—including in moving from shallow to deeper integration measures—refers to the sequencing of reform.[34] This issue was first considered in the 1980s in discussions dealing with the Southern Cone (Argentina, Chile, and Uruguay) experiences and emphasized the macroeconomic consequences of alternative sequences. In particular, this debate asked whether capital controls—arguably the fundamental element of deep integration—should be relaxed before, jointly, or after trade barriers had been reduced. Recent discussions on the experiences of the former communist

32. See, for example, Ito (1993), for a discussion on the U.S. political pressure for economic liberalization in East Asia.

33. See, for example, McKinnon (1991).

34. McKinnon (1991).

nations have broadened the debate and have asked how privatization and other basic institutional reforms should be timed in the effort to move toward market orientation.

The behavior of the real exchange rate is at the heart of the policy debate on the sequence of trade barriers and capital control liberalization. The central issue is that relaxing capital controls would, under some conditions, result in large capital inflows, a large current account deficit, and an appreciation of the real exchange rate.[35] The problem is that an appreciation of the real exchange rate will send the "wrong" signal to the real sector, frustrating the reallocation of resources called for by the trade reform. The effects of this real exchange rate appreciation will be particularly serious if, as argued by Ronald McKinnon and Sebastian Edwards, the transitional period is characterized by "abnormally" high capital inflows that result in temporary real appreciations.[36] If, however, the opening of the capital account is postponed, the real sector will be able to adjust and the new allocation of resources will be consolidated. According to this view, only at this time should the capital account be liberalized.

According to traditional manuals on "how to liberalize," a large devaluation should constitute the first step in a trade reform process. Jagdish Bhagwati and Anne Krueger have pointed out that in the presence of quotas and import licenses a (real) exchange rate depreciation will reduce the rents received by importers, shifting relative prices in favor of export-oriented activities and, thus, reducing the extent of the anti-export bias.[37]

Maintaining a depreciated and competitive real exchange rate during a trade liberalization process is also important to avoid an explosion in imports growth and a balance of payments crisis. Under most circumstances a reduction in the extent of protection will tend to generate a rapid and immediate surge in imports. However, the expansion of exports usually takes some time. Consequently, there is a danger that a trade liberalization reform will generate a large trade balance disequilibrium in the short run. This, however, will not happen if there is a depreciated real exchange rate that encourages

35. This would be the case if the opening of the capital account is done in the context of an overall liberalization program, where the country becomes attractive for foreign investors and speculators. See McKinnon (1982); Edwards (1984); Harberger (1985).

36. McKinnon (1982); Edwards (1984).

37. See Krueger (1978, 1981); and Michaely, Choksi, and Papageorgiou (1991).

exports and helps maintain imports in check. Many countries have historically failed to sustain a depreciated real exchange rate during the transition. Although historically this failure has mainly been the result of expansionary macroeconomic (fiscal) policies that generate speculation and international reserves losses, in some instances large capital inflows have contributed to the real exchange rate over-valuation syndrome.

Korean policymakers and economists have been very apprehensive about the possible effect of the relaxation of capital controls on the real exchange rate. Yung Chul Park and Won Am Park, for example, have recently constructed a simulation model to evaluate the real exchange rate impact of opening the capital account on Korea's real exchange rate.[38] They argue that recent (and rather timid) attempts to slowly relax some of the controls to capital mobility in Korea have resulted in a dramatic increase in speculative activities. According to them this has, in turn, generated a rapid and somewhat artificial real estate boom that has had negative consequences on investment in machinery and equipment. Overall, Park and Park conclude that, under most circumstances, a rapid capital market liberalization would have a large effect on real exchange rates and would have a substantial negative effect on Korea's competitiveness.

The Latin American trade liberalization episodes of the late 1980s and early 1990s were supplemented, at least initially, by active efforts at generating significant real exchange rate depreciations. These competitive real exchange rates were at the center of the vigorous performance of most of Latin America's export sectors during the late 1980s and early 1990s. However, during 1992–94 and largely as a result of very significant increases in capital inflows, most Latin countries have experienced significant real exchange rate appreciations and losses in competitiveness. In a series of important contributions Guillermo A. Calvo, Leonardo Leiderman, and Carmen M. Reinhart have dealt with the capital inflows problem and argued that the concomitant real appreciations (and losses in international competitiveness) have generated considerable concern among policymakers and political leaders.[39] An interesting feature of the recent capital movements is that a large proportion corresponds to portfolio invest-

38. Park and Park (forthcoming).
39. Calvo, Leiderman, and Reinhart (1993; forthcoming).

ment and relatively little is direct foreign investment. Mexico was the most important recipient of foreign funds in that region during the early 1990s. However, as the Mexican peso crisis of December of 1994 painfully showed, large inflows of short-term capital can be easily reversed, especially if the country in question runs a very large current account deficit and is affected by negative political disturbances. A number of authors, most prominently Ron McKinnon, have argued that if Mexico had maintained tight capital controls—that is, if it had stayed away from the seduction of (some forms of) deep integration—the crisis would never have occurred.

Chile tackled the capital inflows problem of the 1980s by implementing a broad set of measures, including the management of exchange rate policy relative to a three-currency basket, imposing reserve requirements on capital inflows, allowing the nominal exchange rate to appreciate somewhat, and undertaking significant sterilization operations. In spite of this multifront approach, Chile has not avoided real exchange rate pressures. Between December of 1991 and December 1992 the Chilean-U.S. bilateral real exchange rate appreciated by approximately 10 percent. As a result, exporters and agriculture producers have been mounting increasing pressure on the government for special treatment, arguing that an implicit contract had been broken by allowing the real exchange rate to appreciate. This type of political reaction is, in fact, becoming more and more generalized throughout the region, adding a difficult social dimension to the real exchange rate issue.

Although there is no easy way to handle the real appreciation pressures, historical experience shows that there are, at least, two possible avenues that the authorities can follow. First, in those countries where the dominant force behind real exchange rate movements is price inertia in the presence of nominal exchange rate anchor policies, the adoption of a pragmatic crawling peg system will usually help. This means that, to some extent, the inflationary targets will have to be less ambitious as a periodic exchange rate adjustment will result in some inflation.[40] However, to the extent that this policy is supplemented by tight overall fiscal policy there should be no concern regarding inflationary explosions.

40. More specifically, with this option the one-digit inflationary goal will be postponed.

Second, the discrimination between short-term (speculative) capital and longer-term capital should go a long way in helping resolve the preoccupations regarding the effects of capital movements on real exchange rates. To the extent that short-term capital flows are more volatile, and thus capital inflows are genuinely long term, especially if they help finance investment projects in the tradables sector, the change in the RER will be a "true equilibrium" phenomenon and should be recognized as such by implementing the required adjustment resource allocation. In practice, however, discriminating between "permanent" and "transitory" capital inflows is difficult; at the end policymakers are forced to make a judgment call. It is highly likely, however, that as a consequence of the Mexican crisis of December 1994, more and more countries will adopt a "defensive stance" in the next few years, either postponing the relaxation of capital controls or, in some cases, even hiking them to new levels.

Appendix A

The Developing Countries, Regional Groupings

I N chapter 2, table 2-1, the countries are grouped as follows in the developing world.

In the terms-of-trade index:

Western Hemisphere: Argentina, Brazil, Chile, Mexico, Paraguay, Uruguay, Bolivia, Colombia, Ecuador, Peru, Venezuela, Costa Rica, El Salvador, Guatemala, Honduras, Nicaragua, Bahamas, Barbados, Belize, Guyana, Jamaica, Trinidad and Tobago, Antigua and Barbuda, Dominica, Grenada, Montserrat, Saint Kitts and Nevis, Saint Lucia, Saint Vincent and the Grenadines, Bermuda, British Virgin Islands, Cayman Islands, Cuba, Dominican Republic, Falkland Islands, French Guiana, Greenland, Guadeloupe, Haiti, Martinique, Netherlands Antilles, Panama, Puerto Rico, Saint Pierre and Miquelon, Suriname, and Turks and Caicos Islands.

Africa: (North) Algeria, Morocco, Tunisia, Egypt, Libya, Sudan; *(other)* Cameroon, Central African Republic, Chad, Congo, Equatorial Guinea, Gabon, Guinea, Liberia, Sierra Leone, Benin, Burkina Faso, Cote d'Ivoire, Mali, Mauritania, Niger, Senegal, Cape Verde, Gambia, Ghana, Guinea-Bissau, Nigeria, Togo, Burundi, Rwanda, Zaire, Angola, Botswana, Comoros, Djibouti, Ethiopia, Kenya, Lesotho, Madagascar, Malawi, Mauritius, Mozambique, Namibia, Reunion, Saint Helena, Sao Tome and Principe, Seychelles, Somalia, Swaziland, Uganda, United Republic of Tanzania, Zambia, and Zimbabwe.

Asia: (West) Bahrain, Kuwait, Oman, Qatar, Saudi Arabia, United Arab Emirates, Cyprus, Iran, Iraq, Jordan, Lebanon, Syria, Turkey, Yemen.

(South and South East) Brunei, Indonesia, Malaysia, Philippines, Singapore, Thailand, Bangladesh, India, Korea, Laos, Sri Lanka, Afghanistan, Bhutan, Cambodia, East Timor, Hong Kong, Macau, Maldives, Myammar, Nepal, Pakistan, and Taiwan.[1]

For LDC export growth:

Western Hemisphere: Antigua and Barbuda, Argentina, Bahamas, Barbados, Belize, Bermuda, Bolivia, Brazil, British Virgin Islands, Cayman Islands, Chile, Colombia, Costa Rica, Cuba, Dominica, Dominican Republic, Ecuador, El Salvador, Falkland Islands, French Guiana, Greenland, Grenada, Guadeloupe, Guatemala, Guyana, Haiti, Honduras, Jamaica, Martinique, Mexico, Montserrat, Netherlands Antilles, Nicaragua, Panama, Paraguay, Peru, Saint Kitts and Nevis, Saint Lucia, Saint Pierre and Miquelon, Saint Vincent and the Grenadines, Suriname, Trinidad and Tobago, Uruguay, and Venezuela.

Africa: Algeria, Egypt, Libya, Morocco, Sudan, Tunisia, Angola, Benin, Botswana, Burkina Faso, Burundi, Cameroon, Cape Verde, Central African Republic, Chad, Comoros, Congo, Cote d'Ivoire, Djibouti, Equatorial Guinea, Ethiopia, Gabon, Gambia, Ghana, Guinea, Guinea-Bissau, Kenya, Lesotho, Liberia, Madagascar, Malawi, Mali, Mauritania, Mauritius, Mozambique, Namibia, Niger, Nigeria, Reunion, Rwanda, Sao Tome and Principe, Senegal, Seychelles, Sierra Leone, Somalia, Swaziland, Togo, Uganda, United Republic of Tanzania, Zaire, Zambia, and Zimbabwe.

Asia: Bahrain, Cyprus, Iran, Iraq, Jordan, Kuwait, Lebanon, Oman, Qatar, Saudi Arabia, Syria, Turkey, United Arab Emirates, Yemen, Afghanistan, Bangladesh, Brunei, Cambodia, Hong Kong, India, Indonesia, Laos, Macau, Malaysia, Maldives, Myammar, Nepal, Pakistan, Philippines, South Korea, Singapore, Sri Lanka, Taiwan, and Thailand.

Europe: Malta, Yugoslavia, Albania, Bulgaria, Czechoslovakia, Germany (former German Democratic Republic), Hungary, Poland, Romania, and the USSR (former).[2]

For the net transfers to developing countries:

Africa: Benin, Botswana, Burkina Faso, Burundi, Cameroon, Cape Verde, Central African Republic, Chad, Comoros, Congo, Cote d'Ivoire, Djibouti, Equatorial Guinea, Ethiopia, Gabon, Gambia, Ghana, Guinea, Guinea-Bissau, Kenya, Lesotho, Liberia, Madagas-

---

1. UNCTAD (1992b, p. 46).
2. UNCTAD (1992a, pp. 2–5).

car, Malawi, Mali, Mauritania, Mauritius, Niger, Nigeria, Rwanda, Sao Tome and Principe, Senegal, Seychelles, Sierra Leone, Somalia, Sudan, Swaziland, Tanzania, Togo, Uganda, Zaire, Zambia, and Zimbabwe.

East Asia and the Pacific: China, Fiji, Hong Kong, Indonesia, Korea, Malaysia, Papua New Guinea, Philippines, Singapore, Solomon Islands, Thailand, Vanatu, and Western Samoa.

Europe and the Mediterranean: Cyprus, Greece, Hungary, Israel, Malta, Portugal, Romania, Turkey, and Yugoslavia.

Europe and Central Asia: Bulgaria, Cyprus, Czechoslovakia, Former Soviet Union, Hungary, Malta, Poland, Portugal, Romania, Turkey, and Yugoslavia.[3]

Latin America and the Caribbean: Argentina, Bahamas, Barbados, Belize, Bolivia, Brazil, Chile, Colombia, Costa Rica, Dominican Republic, Ecuador, El Salvador, Grenada, Guatemala, Guyana, Haiti, Honduras, Jamaica, Mexico, Nicaragua, Panama, Paraguay, Peru, St. Vincent, Trinidad and Tobago, Uruguay, and Venezuela.

North Africa and the Middle East: Algeria, Egypt, Jordan, Lebanon, Morocco, Oman, Syria, Tunisia, Yemen, and North Yemen.

South Asia: Bangladesh, Burma, India, Maldives, Nepal, Pakistan, and Sri Lanka.

---

3. In 1992–93 the grouping Europe and the Mediterranean became Europe and Central Asia. World Bank (1987, pp. 77–105; 1993c, pp. 170–97).

Appendix B

Reforms of Laws Governing Intellectual Property Rights, Selected Latin American Countries

A s discussed in chapter 4, the following regions and nations in Latin America have undertaken reforms of laws governing intellectual property rights. Political difficulties in the Latin American countries often put their governments at odds with the deep integration agenda of the United States.[1]

Andean Pact Countries

The 1991 intellectual property law (Decision 313) improves patent and trademark protection, but the United States complains of inadequacies including compulsory licensing, limited patent and trademark terms, working requirements, and lack of transitional ("pipeline") protection. New Decisions in 1993 (344 and 345) respond in part to U.S. concerns, but Colombia, Peru, and Venezuela were still cited in 1994 for inadequate protection.

Argentina

New patent law introduced to Congress in 1991, but the United States continues to protest certain provisions and subjects the country to Special 301 review in 1993. The 1993 decrees raised copyright

1. See Hufbauer and Schott (1994, pp. 143–45); U.S. Trade Representative (1994, pp. 8, 22–24, 40–41, 61, 203, 275).

protection to Berne standards and extended copyright protection to computer software and databases, but patent law languishes in Congress.

Brazil

Intellectual property cited in 1988 Super 301 action, but the United States suspends action in 1990 after new Color government promises to submit a new intellectual property rights bill. Proposed bill falls short of U.S. demands in several respects, and congressional amendments weaken it further, leading to sharp confrontation with the United States in 1993–94.

Chile

The 1991 law on intellectual property revised previous patent and trademark law, although the United States still complains about inadequate patent protection. The 1992 revision of copyright law adopts Berne Convention standards.

Mexico

The 1987 amendments to the 1976 law on inventions and trademarks strengthen protection for patents, trademarks, copyrights, and trade secrets, but implementation in some areas was delayed until 1997. The United States is not satisfied and withdraws some benefits of the Generalized System of Preferences in 1987 and places Mexico on the priority watch list in 1988. In 1990 the Salinas administration announces its intention to introduce new legislation. This comprehensive copyright and patent law revision, passed in 1991, lays the foundation for very strong NAFTA rules that exceed Uruguay Round standards in several respects. The United States continues to complain of lax enforcement.

Appendix C

Nontrade and Deep Integration Measures in NAFTA

As discussed in chapter 4 the following issues, negotiated in NAFTA, will be of primary concern to developing countries as they grapple with the deep integration agenda in the future.[1]

Investment

—*General.* NAFTA investors will receive the more favorable of national or most favored nation treatment, unless specific exceptions are requested by states, provinces and local governments. All new performance requirements are prohibited, and most existing ones are to be phased out over ten years. Investors have the right of access to foreign exchange for the purpose of profit and capital repatriation. Expropriation without compensation is forbidden, and compensation must be at fair market value. Certain sectoral and functional restrictions remain in place, as does Mexico's right to screen acquisitions over certain thresholds.

—*Taxation.* Bilateral tax treaty between the United States and Mexico signed in September 1992 reduces withholding taxes on interest, dividends, and royalty payments.

—*Energy.* Though PEMEX is allowed to retain a monopoly on oil exploration and development, gasoline and fuel oil sales, NAFTA lifts investment restrictions on fourteen of nineteen basic petrochemicals, certain electric-generating facilities, and new coal mines.

1. See Hufbauer and Schott (1993, pp. 120–153, 178–85).

146

—*Financial services.* The agreement initiates a gradual phase-out of restrictions on foreign ownership of financial services, subject to various interim safeguards. These include foreign market share caps, individual market share caps, and the right to freeze new acquisitions in banking, equity limits, and market share caps on new insurance entrants, and foreign and individual market share caps in the brokerage industry.

—*Telecommunications.* Agreement maintains Mexican restrictions on radio and television ownership and investment in the provision of basic local and long-distance telephone services, though the latter provision in part protects foreign investors in the newly privatized TELMEX. Mexico will lift restrictions on value-added information services.

—*Transportation.* Eases some restrictions on investment in bus and trucking services and land-side aspects of port activities but maintains Mexican prohibition on foreign investment in railroads.

Regulatory Reform and Standards

The following provisions are made for regulatory reform and standards.

—*Transportation.* NAFTA partners agree to harmonize technical and safety standards with respect to motor carrier and rail operations. Nonmedical standards will be compatible 1.5 years after NAFTA enters into force; medical standards 2.5 years after.

—*Telecommunications.* North American firms will have access to the use of public telecommunication networks and services on a reasonable, nondiscriminatory, and cost-oriented basis and will be allowed to operate private intracorporate communications networks.

—*Government procurement.* Modeled on the GATT Government Procurement Code, Mexico makes a commitment to phase out procurement restrictions over ten years. Exceptions are substantial and include transport services, public utilities, research and development, and basic communications.

Intellectual property

—*Copyrights.* Calls for adherence to the Berne Convention standards but also extends protection to computer programs and databases. Gives copyright owners of computer programs and sound recordings the right to prohibit rental. Establishes fifty-year term for sound recording and motion pictures.

—*Trademarks.* Requires registration, initially for ten years renewable for successive terms of not less than ten years. Prohibits compulsory licensing or mandatory linking of trademarks.

—*Patents.* Limits ability of NAFTA countries to impose compulsory licensing. Protects patents for a minimum of twenty years and establishes "pipeline" protection for patents awaiting approval. Grants patent protection for pharmaceuticals and agricultural chemicals, as well as exclusive use of proprietary data required for the approval process of these products, but excludes biotechnical inventions and diagnostic, therapeutic, and surgical methods.

Environment

Maintains existing standards at all levels of government and allows a country to prohibit goods that do not meet those standards but does not explicitly address process standards. Explicitly states that parties may enact tougher standards. Requires that technical standards have a scientific basis and allows countries to impose environmental standards on foreign investors, but the standards must be imposed in a nondiscriminatory fashion (see dispute settlement).

Labor

The original NAFTA contains no explicit commitments on labor standards, although a May 1991 memo of understanding and a September 1992 agreement to establish a consultative commission on labor matters provided encouragement for Mexico to upgrade its labor laws (see dispute settlement).

Dispute Settlement and Institutions

NAFTA extends dispute settlement procedures of the U.S.-Canada Agreement to Mexico, establishes a trilateral North American Free Trade Commission composed of cabinet-level representatives, and establishes a dispute settlement process consisting of the following steps:

1. Consultations, with a time limit for resolution of the dispute within thirty to forty-five days.

2. If these fail, any country can call a meeting of the commission to use its good offices, mediation, or conciliation.

3. If this fails, the complaining party can bring the dispute to a GATT or a NAFTA panel. The panel will consist of private sector experts and will issue a final report within 120 days. Disputing parties are called on to comply in a timely fashion, and if they do not, parties are allowed to suspend trade benefits.

4. Once a panel decision has been made, either country may request a three-person extraordinary-challenge committee that will uphold or overturn the panel ruling. In the latter case, a new panel will be set up.

—*Dumping and Subsidies.* The procedure for review of antidumping (AD) and countervailing duty (CVD) actions is similar to the general dispute settlement mechanism, including binding panel decisions and the option of calling for an extraordinary challenge committee. In addition, however, a country may request a special committee to determine whether a country's domestic law has undermined the functioning of the panel system. NAFTA allows members to retain their AD/CVD laws, but any changes may be subject to panel review. Moreover, Mexico agreed in an annex to undertake reforms to provide full due process guarantees and judicial review to U.S. exporters for AD/CVD cases.

—*Investment.* A NAFTA investor can seek binding arbitral rulings in an international forum and can go to court in any of the three countries for enforcement of arbitral awards.

—*Environment.* The North American Agreement on Environmental Cooperation (the environment side-agreement) establishes a Commission on Environmental Cooperation, with a Joint Public Advisory Committee of five nongovernmental members from each country. Any organization or individual may issue a complaint, or submission, that a NAFTA member is not enforcing its national laws. Establishes a procedure that includes the following:

1. Development of a factual record by the secretariat as the basis for consultations.

2. If the matter is not resolved within sixty days, the complainant can call for a meeting of the council.

3. If the council cannot resolve the dispute, an arbitration panel may be established with an affirmative vote of two of the three

members. The panel's final report must be prepared within 240 days. If the panel finds that a party has not upheld its laws, the parties then agree on an action plan. If the parties cannot agree on an action plan, they reconvene to consider the plan proposed by the party accused of wrongdoing. The panel will either accept the plan or propose its own.

4. If the plan is not fully implemented, an arbitration panel will determine a fine.

5. Trade sanctions will only be allowed if the country accused fails to pay the fine and continues to inadequately enforce its laws.

—Labor. The Commission on Labor Cooperation parallels the Commission on Environmental Cooperation but lacks nongovernmental representation; rather, it will be serviced by three national administrative offices and by an evaluation committee of experts on domestic labor laws. The dispute settlement mechanism is broadly similar to that for the environment except that complaints must first go through national administrative offices; if it is not resolved there, than it will be referred to the council and the evaluation committee of experts.

Complaints may be brought in any of eleven areas, but the procedures for dispute resolution vary among them. Only offenses in the occupational health and safety, child labor, and minimum wage areas can ultimately carry fines and sanctions. Migrant workers, forced labor, employment discrimination, equal pay for men and women, and compensation for accident and occupational diseases are subject to review by the council and independent experts. The right to strike, the right to bargain collectively, and the right to organize can only be reviewed by the ministers.

References

Aaron, Henry, and others. 1993. "Integrating the World Economy: General Themes." Memo. Brookings.

Abreu, Marcelo de Paiva, and Winston Fritsch. 1989. "Market Access for Manufactured Exports." In *Developing Countries and the Global Trading System,* edited by John Whalley, 112–31. London: Macmillan.

Aggarwal, Vinod K. 1992. "The Political Economy of Service Sector Negotiations in the Uruguay Round." *Fletcher Forum* 16 (Winter): 35–54.

Ahluwalia, Montek S. 1994. "India's Quiet Economic Revolution." *Columbia Journal of World Business* 29 (Spring): 6–12.

Aho, C. Michael, and Sylvia Ostry. 1990. "Regional Trading Blocs: Pragmatic or Problematic Policy?" In *The Global Economy: America's Role in the Decade Ahead,* edited by William E. Brock and Robert D. Hormats, 147–73. W.W. Norton.

Alam, Asad, and Sarath Rajapatirana. 1993. "Trade Reform in Latin America and the Caribbean." *Finance and Development* 30 (September): 44–47.

Amato, Theresa A. 1990. "Labor Rights Conditionality: United States Trade Legislation and the International Legal Order." *New York University Law Review* 65 (April): 79–125.

Amsden, Alice. 1989. *Asia's Next Giant.* Oxford University Press.

Anderson, Kym, and Hege Norheim. 1993. "History, Geography and Regional Economic Integration." In *Regional Integration and the Global Trading System,* edited by Kym Anderson and Richard Blackhurst, 19–51. Harvester Wheatsheaf.

Arellano, José Pablo, and others. 1982. *Modelo Económico Chileno: Trayectoria de una Crítica.* Santiago: Editorial Aconcagua.

Arellano, Rogelio. 1989. "On the Causes and Consequences of Real Exchange Rate Variability: A Comparative Analysis of the East Asian and Latin American Experiences." Ph.D. dissertation, University of California, Los Angeles, Department of Economics.

151

Asia-Pacific Economic Cooperation. 1993. *A Vision for APEC: Towards an Asia Pacific Economic Community: Report of the Eminent Persons Group to APEC Ministers.* Singapore: Asia-Pacific Economic Cooperation.

———. 1994. Achieving the APEC Vision: Free and Open Trade in the Asia-Pacific: Second Report of the Eminent Persons Group. Singapore: APEC.

Baker, Mark D., and Mark D. Holmes. 1991. "An Analysis of Latin American Foreign Investment Law: Proposals for Striking a Balance between Foreign Investment and Political Stability." *Inter-American Law Review* 23 (Fall): 1–38.

Balassa, Bela. 1988. "Outward Orientation." In Hollis Chenery and T. N. Srinivasan, eds., *Handbook of Development Economics,* vol. 2, 1645–89. Amsterdam: North-Holland.

Balassa, Bela, and John Williamson. 1990. *Adjusting to Success: Balance of Payments Policy in the East Asian NICs.* Washington: Institute for International Economics. April.

Ball, Nicole. 1992. *Pressing for Peace: Can Aid Induce Reform?* Washington: Overseas Development Council.

Bates, Robert, and Anne O. Krueger, eds. 1993. *Political and Economic Interactions in Economic Policy Reform.* Cambridge: Blackwell.

Bello, Judith Hipler, and Alan F. Holmer. 1990. "The Heart of the 1988 Trade Act: A Legislative History of the Amendments to Section 301." In *Aggressive Unilateralism: America's 301 Trade Policy and the World Trading System,* edited by Jagdish Bhagwati and Hugh Patrick, 49–89. University of Michigan Press.

Bergsten, C. Fred. 1994. "APEC: the Bogor Declaration and the Path Ahead." Washington: Institute for International Economics.

Bhagwati, Jagdish. 1978. *Foreign Trade Regimes and Economic Development: Anatomy and Consequences of Exchange Control Regimes.* Cambridge, Mass.: Ballinger.

———. 1984. "Splintering and Disembodiment of Service and Developing Countries." *World Economy* 7 (June 1984): 133–44.

———. 1990. "Aggressive Unilateralism: An Overview." In *Aggressive Unilateralism: America's 301 Trade Policy and the World Trading System,* edited by Jagdish Bhagwati and Hugh Patrick, 1–45. University of Michigan Press.

———. 1993. "Regionalism and Multilateralism: An Overview." In *New Dimensions in Regional Integration,* edited by Jaime de Melo and Arvind Panagariya, 22–57. Cambridge University Press.

Bhagwati, Jagdish, and Hugh Patrick, eds. 1990. *Aggressive Unilateralism: America's 301 Trade Policy and the World Trading System.* University of Michigan Press.

Bianchi, Andres, and Takahashi Nohara, eds., 1988. *A Comparative Study on Economic Development between Asia and Latin America.* Tokyo: Institute of Developing Economies.

Black, Dorothy J. 1992. "International Trade v. Environmental Protection: The Case of the U.S. Embargo on Mexican Tuna." *Law and Policy in International Business* 24 (Fall): 123–56.

Boeker, Paul H. ed., 1993. *Latin America's Turnaround: Privatization, Foreign Investment and Growth.* San Francisco: ICS Press.

Boeninger, Edgardo. 1991. "Governance and Development: Issues and Constraints." *Proceedings of the World Bank Annual Conference on Development Economics,* 267–88. Washington.: World Bank.

Boltuck, Richard, and Robert E. Litan, eds. 1991. *Down in the Dumps: Administration of the Unfair Trade Laws.* Brookings.

Bowie, Alisdair. 1994. "The Dynamics of Business-Government Relations in Industrializing Malaysia." In *Business and Government in Industrializing East and Southeast Asia,* edited by Andrew MacIntyre, 167–94. Cornell University Press.

Bresnan, John. 1993. *Managing Indonesia: The Modern Political Economy.* Columbia University Press.

Bresser Pereira and others. 1993. *Economic Reform in New Democracies: A Social-Democratic Approach.* Cambridge University Press.

Brown, Drusilla, Alan V. Deardorff, and Robert M. Stern. 1993. "International Labor Standards and Trade: A Theoretical Analysis." Discussion Paper 333. University of Michigan, Institute of Public Policy.

Bryant, Ralph. Forthcoming. *International Coordination of National Stabilization Policies.* Brookings.

Bush, George. 1991. "Remarks Announcing the Enterprise for the Americas Initiative." In *Public Papers of the Presidents of the United States: George Bush, 1990,* Book One, 873–77. Government Printing Office.

Calvo, Guillermo, A. Leonardo Leiderman, and Carmen Reinhart. 1993. "Capital Inflows and Real Exchange Rate Appreciation in Latin America: The Role of External Factors." *IMF Staff Papers,* vol. 40. (March): 108–51.

———. Forthcoming. "Capital Inflows Latin America with Reference to the Asian Experience." In Sebastian Edwards, ed., *Capital Controls, Exchange Rates and Monetary Policy in the World Economy.* Cambridge University Press.

Carbaugh, Robert, and Darwin Wassink. 1992. "Environmental Standards and International Competitiveness." *World Competition* 16 (September): 81–90.

Cardenas, Emilio. 1992. "The Treaty of Asuncion: A Southern Cone Common Market (Mercosur) Begins to Take Shape." *World Competition* 16 (June): 65–77.

CEPAL (Comisión Económica para América Latina). 1992. *Balance Preliminar de la Economía de América Latina y el Caribe.* Santiago: CEPAL.

Charnovitz, Steve. 1992. "Environmental and Labour Standards in International Trade." *World Economy* 15 (September): 335–56.

———. 1993. "Environmental Trade Measures: Multilateral or Unilateral?" *Environmental Policy and Law* 23 (3–4): 154–59.

Cheit, Earl. 1992. "A Declaration on Open Regionalism in the Pacific." *California Management Review* 35 (Fall 1992): 116–30.

Cheng, Tun-jen. 1993. "Guarding the Commanding Heights: The State as Banker in Taiwan." In *The Politics of Finance in Developing Countries,* edited by Stephan Haggard, Chung Lee, and Sylvia Maxfield, 55–92. Cornell University Press.

Chia, Siow Yue, and Tsao Yuan Lee. 1993. "Subregional Economic Zones: A New Motive Force in Asia-Pacific Development." In *Pacific Dynamism and the*

International Economic System, edited by C. Fred Bergsten and Marcus Noland, 225–72. Washington: Institute for International Economics.

Cho, Yoon-je. 1987. "How the United States Broke into Korea's Insurance Market." *World Economy* 10 (December) 483–96.

Choi, Byung-Sun. 1993. "Financial Policy and Big Business in Korea: The Perils of Financial Regulation." In *The Politics of Finance in Developing Countries*, edited by Stephan Haggard, Chung Lee, and Sylvia Maxfield, 23–54. Cornell University Press.

Cline, W. R. 1983. "Reciprocity: A New Approach to World Trade Policy?" In *Trade Policy in the 1980s*, edited by W.R. Cline, 121–58. Washington: Institute for International Economics.

Commission of the European Communities. 1982. "Memorandum on the Community's Development Policy." Supplement 5/82 to the *Bulletin of the European Communities*. Office of the Official Publications of the European Communities. Luxembourg.

Cortazar, René. 1982. "Precios y Remuneraciones." In José Pablo Arellano and others, *Modelo Económica Chileno: Trayectoria de una Critica*, 290–92. Santiago: Editorial Aconcagua.

Cosgrove, Carol, and Pierre-Henri Laurent. 1992. "The Unique Relationship: The European Community and the ACP." In *The External Relations of the European Community: The International Response to 1992*, edited by John Redmond, 120–37. St. Martin's Press.

Council for Economic Planning and Development. 1993. *Taiwan Statistical Data Book*. Taibei, Republic of China.

Cowhey, Peter. 1994. "Pacific Trade Relations after the Cold War: GATT, NAFTA, ASEAN and APEC." University of California, San Diego.

Cowhey, Peter F., and Jonathan D. Aronson. 1993. *Managing the World Economy: The Consequences of Corporate Alliances*. New York: Council on Foreign Relations.

Dandeker, Rebecca D. 1992. "The Rose Garden Agreement: Is Mercosur the Next Step toward Hemispheric Free Trade?" *Law and Policy in International Business* 24 (Fall): 157–80.

Davenport, Michael W.S. 1990. "The External Policy of the Community and Its Effects upon the Manufactured Exports of the Developing Countries." *Journal of Common Market Studies* 29 (December): 183–200.

de la Torre, Augusto, and Margaret R. Kelly. 1992. *Regional Trade Arrangements*. Occasional Paper 93. Washington: International Monetary Fund.

Destler, I. M. 1992. *American Trade Politics*, 2d ed. Washington: Institute for International Economics.

Destler, I. M., John Odell, and Kimberly Ann Elliott. 1987. *Anti-Dumping Protection: Changing Forces in United States Trade Politics*. Washington: Institute for International Economics.

Dinan, Donald R. 1991. "Review of Federal Unfair Competition Actions: Practice and Procedure Under Section 337 of the Tariff Act of 1930." *International Lawyer* 25 (Fall): 777–83.

Doner, Richard. 1993. "Japanese Foreign Investment and the Creation of a Pacific Region." In *Regionalism and Rivalry: Japan and the United States in Pacific Asia,* edited by Jeffrey A. Frankel and Miles Kahler, 159–216. University of Chicago Press.

Doner, Richard, and Anek Laothamatas. 1994. "The Political Economy of Structural Adjustment in Thailand." In *Voting for Reform: Political Liberalization, Democracy and Economic Adjustment,* edited by Stephan Haggard and Steven B. Webb, 411–52. Oxford University Press.

Drake, William J., and Kalypso Nicolaïdes. 1992. "Ideas, Interests and Institutionalization: 'Trade in Services' and the Uruguay Round." *International Organization* 46 (Winter): 37–100.

Drysdale, Peter, and Ross Garnaut. 1993. "The Pacific: An Application of a General Theory of Economic Integration." In C. Fred Bergsten and Marcus Noland, eds., *Pacific Dynamism and the International Economic System,* 183–224. Washington: Institute for International Economics.

Economist Intelligence Unit. 1993. *Investing, Licensing and Trading Abroad: India.* London: Economist Intelligence Unit.

Edwards, Sebastian. 1984. "The Order of Liberalization of the External Sector in Developing Countries." Princeton Essays in International Finance 156. Princeton University.

———. 1989. *Real Exchange Rates, Devaluation, and Adjustment: Exchange Rate Policy in Developing Countries.* MIT Press.

———. 1993. "The Political Economy of Inflation and Stabilization in Developing Countries." NBER Working Paper 4319. Cambridge, Mass.: National Bureau of Economic Research.

———. 1995. *From Despair to Hope: Crisis and Economic Reform in Latin America.* Oxford University Press/World Bank.

Edwards, Sebastian, and Alejandra Edwards. 1991. *Monetarism and Liberalization: The Chilean Experiment.* University of Chicago Press.

Elek, Andrew. 1992a. "Pacific Economic Cooperation: Policy Choices for the 1990s." *Asia Pacific Economic Literature* 6 (May): 1–15.

———. 1992b. "Trade Policy Options for the Asia Pacific Region in the 1990s: The Potential of Open Regionalism." *American Economic Review: Papers and Proceedings* 82 (May): 74–78.

Encarnation, Dennis. 1991. *Rivals beyond Trade: America versus Japan in Global Competition.* Cornell University Press.

Ensign, Margee M. 1992. *Doing Good or Doing Well? Japan's Foreign Aid Program.* Columbia University Press.

Erzan, Refik, and Alexander Yeats. 1992. "U.S.-Latin American Free Trade Areas: Some Empirical Evidence." In *The Premise and the Promise: Free Trade in the Americas,* edited by Sylvia Saborio and others, 117–52. New Brunswick: Transaction Publishers.

Fajnzylber, Fernando. 1990. *Unavoidable Industrial Restructuring in Latin America.* Duke University Press.

Finger, J. Michael. 1993. "A Rock and a Hard Place: The Two Faces of U.S. Trade Policy toward Korea." In *Shaping a New Economic Relationship: The Republic of*

Korea and the United States, edited by Jongryn Mo and Ramon Myers, 65–91. Stanford: Hoover Institution Press.

Finger, J. Michael, H. Keith Hall, and Douglas R. Nelson. 1982. "The Political Economy of Administered Protection." *American Economic Review* 72 (June): 452–66.

Finger, J. Michael, and K.C. Fung. 1993. "Can Competition Policy Control '301'?" Paper prepared for the Research Seminar on Approaches to Competition Policy in International Trade. Hochschule St. Gallen, Switzerland. September 16–18.

Finger, J. Michael, and Tracy Murray. 1990. "Policing Unfair Imports: The U.S. Example." Working Paper WPS 401. Washington: World Bank.

Fishlow, Albert, and Stephan Haggard. 1992. *The United States and the Regionalization of the World Economy.* Paris: Organization for Economic Cooperation and Development, Development Centre.

Fontaine, Arturo. 1992. "Sobre el Pecado Original de la Transformación Capitalista Chilena." In Barry Levine, ed., *El Desafío Neoliberal: El Fin del Tercermundismo en América Latina, 93–139.* Bogota: Editorial Norma.

Fowler, Mark S., and Aileen Amarandos Pisciotta. 1993. "Privatization as an Objective: Telecommunications and Regulatory Reform." In *Latin America's Turnaround: Privatization, Foreign Investment and Growth,* edited by Paul H. Boeker, 115–28 San Francisco: ICS Press.

Foxley, Alejandro. 1982. "Resuelve el Modelo Económico Los Problemas de Fondo?" In Jose Pablo Arrellano and others, *Modelo Económico Chileno: Trayectoria de Una Crítica, 15–33.* Santiago: Editorial Aconcagua.

———. 1983a. "Después del Monetarismo." In Alejandro Foxley, and others, eds., 1–22. *Reconstrucción Económica Para la Democracia.* Santiago: Corporación de Investigaciones Económicas para Latinoamérica (CIEPLAN).

———. 1983b. *Latin American Experiences with Neoconservative Economics.* University of California Press.

Frank, Isaiah. 1979. "The Graduation Issue for the LDCs." *Journal of World Trade Law* 13: 289–302.

Frankel, Jeffrey, and Miles Kahler, eds. 1993. *Regionalism and Rivalry: Japan and the United States in Pacific Asia.* University of Chicago Press.

French, Hilary F. 1993. *Costly Tradeoffs: Reconciling Trade and the Environment.* World Watchpaper 113. Washington: Worldwatch Institute.

GATT. 1993. *GATT Activities 1992.* Geneva.

Greenaway, David. 1991. "Why Are We Negotiating on TRIMs?" In *Global Protectionism,* edited by David Greenaway and others, 145–70. London: Macmillan.

Griffin, Joseph P. 1992. "The Impact of Reconsideration of U.S. Antitrust Policy Intended to Protect U.S. Exporters." *World Competition* 15 (June): 5–14.

Grilli, Enzo R. 1993. *The European Community and the Developing Countries.* Cambridge University Press.

Grinspun, Ricardo, and Maxwell A. Cameron, eds. 1993. *The Political Economy of North American Free Trade.* St. Martins Press.

Guillaumont, Patrick, and Sylviane Guillaumont. 1989. "The Implications of European Monetary Union for African Countries." *Journal of Common Market Studies* 28 (December): 139–53.

Guitián, Manuel. Forthcoming. "Capital Account Liberalization: Bringing Policy in Line with Reality." In Sebastian Edwards, ed., *Capital Controls, Exchange Rates and Monetary Policy in the World Economy.* Cambridge University Press.

Haggard, Stephan. 1986. "The Politics of Adjustment: Lessons from the IMF's Extended Fund Facility." In *The Politics of International Debt,* edited by Miles Kahler, 157–86. Cornell University Press.

———. 1990. *Pathways from the Periphery.* Cornell University Press.

———. 1994. "Thinking about Regionalism: The Politics of Minilateralism in Asia and the Americas." Paper prepared for the American Political Science Association annual meeting, New York. September 1–4.

Haggard, Stephan, and Robert R. Kaufman, eds. 1992. *The Politics of Adjustment.* Princeton University Press.

———. Forthcoming. *The Political Economy of Democratic Transitions.* Princeton University Press.

Haggard, Stephan, and Steven B. Webb, eds. 1994. *Voting for Reform: Democracy, Political Liberalization and Economic Adjustment.* Oxford University Press.

Hakim, Peter. 1992. "President Bush's Southern Strategy: The Enterprise for the Americas Initiative." *Washington Quarterly* 15 (Spring): 93–106.

Han, Sun-Taik. 1992. *European Integration: The Impact on Asian Newly Industrializing Economies.* Paris: Organization for Economic Cooperation and Development, Development Centre Documents.

Harberger, Arnold C.. 1985. "Observations on the Chilean Economy, 1973—1983." *Economic Development and Cultural Change* 33 (April): 451–62.

Herzenberg, Stephen, and Jorge F. Perez-Lopez, eds. 1990. *Labor Standards and Development in the Global Economy.* Washington: U.S. Department of Labor, Bureau of International Labor Affairs.

Higgott, Richard, Richard Leaver, and John Ravenhill, eds. 1993. *Pacific Economic Relations in the 1990s: Cooperation or Conflict?* Boulder: Lynne Rienner.

Hufbauer, Gary Clyde, and Jeffrey J. Schott. 1992. *North American Free Trade: Issues and Recommendations.* Washington: Institute for International Economics.

———. 1993. *NAFTA: An Assessment.* Washington: Institute for International Economics.

———. 1994. *Western Hemispheric Integration.* Washington: Institute for International Economics.

Ichimura, Shinichi. 1994. "Regional Integration Issues in Asia." In Korea Economic Institute of America, *Joint Korea-U.S. Academic Symposium,* vol. 4. Washington: Korea Economic Institute of America.

Imada, Pearl, and Seiji Naya. 1992. *AFTA: The Way Ahead.* Singapore: Institute of Southeast Asian Studies.

International Monetary Fund. 1989. *Developments in International Exchange and Trade Systems.* Washington.

———. Various years. *Direction of Trade Statistics Yearbook.* Washington.

———. 1992. *Developments in International Exchange and Payments Systems.* Washington.

———. 1993. *International Financial Statistics Yearbook.* Washington.

Ito, Takatoshi. 1993. "U.S. Political Pressure and Economic Liberalization in East Asia." In Jeffrey Frankel and Miles Kahler, eds., *Regionalism and Rivalry: Japan and the U.S. in Pacific Asia,* 391–422. Chicago: NBER/University of Chicago Press.

Jackson, John H. 1989. *The World Trading System: Law and Policy in International Economic Relations.* MIT Press.

Kahler, Miles. 1990. "Orthodoxy and Its Alternatives: Explaining Approaches to Stabilization and Adjustment." In *Economic Crisis and Policy Choice: The Politics of Adjustment in the Third World,* edited by Joan Nelson, 33–61 Princeton University Press.

———. 1992. "External Influence, Conditionality, and the Politics of Adjustment." In *The Politics of Economic Adjustment,* edited by Stephan Haggard and Robert Kaufman, 89–138. Princeton University Press.

———. 1993. "Trade and Domestic Differences." Paper presented at conference on Domestic Institutions, Trade, and the Pressures for National Convergence, Rockefeller Foundation Study and Conference Center. Bellagio, Italy. February 22–26.

Kahler, Miles, and John Odell. 1989. "Developing Country Coalition-Building and International Trade Negotiations." In *Developing Countries and the Global Trading System,* vol. 1, Thematic Studies from a Ford Foundation Project, edited by John Whalley, 149–67. London: Macmillan.

Kaufman, Robert R., Carlos Bazdresch, and Blanca Heredia. 1994. "Mexico: Radical Reform in a Dominant Party System." In *Voting for Reform: Democracy, Political Liberalization, and Economic Adjustment.* Oxford University Press for the World Bank.

Keohane, Robert. 1984. *After Hegemony: Cooperation and Discord in the World Economy.* Princeton University Press.

Keohane, Robert, and Joseph Nye, Jr. 1975. "International Interdependence and Integration." In *The Handbook of Political Science,* vol. 8, edited by Fred I. Greenstein and Nelson W. Polsby, 363–414. Reading: Addison-Wesley.

Khalizadeh-Shirazi, Javad, and Roberto Zagha. 1994. "Economic Reforms in India: Achievements and the Agenda Ahead." *Columbia Journal of World Business* 29 (Spring 1994): 24–31.

Kiekens, Jean-Pierre. 1993. "Towards Eco-Labelling of Tropical Timber." *Courier* 142 (November-December): 95–96.

Kim, Kwang Suk. 1991. "Korea." In Michael Michaely, Armeane Choksi, and Demetris Papageorgiou, eds., *Liberalizing Foreign Trade in Developing Countries: The Lessons of Experience,* 1–131. Basil Blackwell.

Kingston, Jeff. 1993. "Bolstering the New Order: Japan's ODA Relationship with Indonesia." In *Japan's Foreign Aid: Power and Policy in a New Era,* edited by Bruce Koppel and Robert Orr, Jr., 41–62. Boulder: Westview Press.

Koekkoek, K. A. 1988. "The Integration of Developing Countries in the GATT System." *World Development* 16 (August): 947–57.

Koppel, Bruce M., and Robert M. Orr, Jr., eds. 1993. *Japan's Foreign Aid: Power and Policy in a New Era.* Boulder: Westview Press.

Kramer, Heinz. 1993. "The European Community's Response to the 'New Eastern Europe.'" *Journal of Common Market Studies* 31, (June): 213–44.

Krueger, Anne O. 1978. *Foreign Trade Regimes and Economic Development: Liberalization Attempts and Consequences.* Cambridge, Mass.: National Bureau of Economic Research.

———. 1981. *Trade and Employment in Developing Countries.* University of Chicago Press.

———. 1990. *Perspectives on Trade and Development.* Exeter: Harvester Wheatsheaf.

———. 1992. *Economic Policies at Cross-Purposes: The United States and Developing Countries.* Brookings.

———. Forthcoming. *Trade Policies and Developing Countries.* Brookings.

Krueger, Anne O., Constantine Michalopoulos, and Vernon Ruttan. 1989. *Aid and Development.* Johns Hopkins University Press.

Krugman, Paul. 1989. "A Model of Balance of Payments Crises." *Journal of Money, Credit, and Banking* 11 (1979): 311–25.

———. 1991. "Is Bilateralism Bad?" In *International Trade and Trade Policy,* edited by Elhanan Helpman and Assaf Razin, 9–23. MIT Press.

Lawrence, Robert Z. 1992. "Emerging Regional Arrangements: Building Blocks or Stumbling Blocks?" In *Finance and the International Economy,* vol. 5, edited by R. O'Brien, 22–35. Oxford University Press.

———. Forthcoming. *Regionalism, Multilateralism, and Deeper Integration.* Brookings.

Lewis, John P. 1992. *Pro-Poor Aid Conditionality.* Washington: Overseas Development Council.

Lin, Ching-Yuan. 1988. "East Asia and Latin America as Contrasting Models." *Economic Development and Cultural Change* 36 (April): S153–97.

Lincoln, Edward J. 1992. "Japan's Rapidly Emerging Strategy toward Asia." Technical Paper 38. Paris: OECD Development Centre.

———. 1993. *Japan's New Global Role.* Brookings.

Liu, Lawrence S. 1990. "Legal and Policy Perspectives on United States Trade Initiatives and Economic Liberalization in the Republic of China." *Michigan Journal of International Law* 11 (Winter 1990): 326–67.

Low, Patrick. 1993. *Trading Free: The GATT and U.S. Trade Policy.* New York: Twentieth Century Fund Press.

Low, Patrick, and Alexander Yeats. 1992. "Do 'Dirty' Industries Migrate?" In Discussion Paper 159, *International Trade and the Environment,* 89–103. Washington: World Bank.

Luedde-Neurath, Richard. 1986. *Import Controls and Export-Oriented Development: A Reassessment of the South Korean Case.* Boulder: Westview Press.

Lumsdaine, David H. 1993. *Moral Vision in International Politics: The Foreign Aid Regime 1949–1989.* Princeton University Press.

Lustig, Nora. 1992. *Mexico: The Remaking of an Economy.* Brookings.

Lustig, Nora, Barry P. Bosworth, and Robert Z. Lawrence. 1992. *North American Free Trade: Assessing the Impact.* Brookings.

MacIntyre, Andrew, ed. 1994. *Business and Government in Industrializing Asia.* Cornell University Press.

Mack, Andrew, and John Ravenhill, eds. 1994. *Pacific Cooperation: Building Economic and Security Regimes in the Asia-Pacific Region.* St. Leonards, Australia: Allen and Unwin.

McKinnon, Ronald. 1982. "The Order of Economic Liberalization: Lessons from Chile and Argentina." *Carnegie-Rochester Conference Series on Public Policy* 17. Amsterdam: North-Holland.

————. 1991. *The Order of Economic Liberalization: Financial Control in the Transition to a Market Economy.* Johns Hopkins University Press.

McMillan, John. 1994. "Why Does Japan Resist Foreign Market-Opening Pressure?" University of California, San Diego.

Matthews, Alan, and Dermot McAleese. 1990. "LDC Primary Exports to the EC: Prospects Post-1992." *Journal of Common Market Studies* 29 (December): 157–80.

Maxfield, Sylvia. 1993. "The Politics of Central Banking in Developing Countries." Yale University.

Meller, Patricio. 1984. "Los Chicago Boys y el Modelo Economico Chileno: 1973—1983." *Corporacion de Investigaciones Economicas para Latinoamerica* 43 (January): 1–22.

Michaely, Michael, Armeane Choksi, and Demetris Papageorgiou, eds. 1991. *Liberalizing Foreign Trade.* Basil Blackwell.

Milner, Helen. 1988. *Resisting the Protectionist Temptation.* Princeton University Press.

Mody, Ashoka. 1990. "New International Environment for Intellectual Property Rights." In *Intellectual Property Rights in Science, Technology, and Economic Performance,* edited by Francis Rushing and Carole Ganz Brown, 203–39. Boulder: Westview Press.

Mosley, Paul, Jane Harrigan, and John Toye. 1992. *Aid and Power: The World Bank and Policy-Based Lending.* London: Routledge.

Mumme, Stephen P. 1993. "Environmentalists, NAFTA and North American Environmental Management." *Journal of Environment and Development* 2 (Winter 1993): 205–20.

Mutti, John. 1993. "Intellectual Property Protection in the United States under Section 337." *World Economy* 16 (May):339–57.

Naim, Moises. 1993. *Paper Tigers and Minotaurs.* Washington: Carnegie Endowment.

————. 1994. "Latin America's Journey to the Market: From Macroeconomic Shocks to Institutional Therapy." Paper presented at the conference on Economic Reform and Democracy. International Forum for Democratic Studies, Washington, May 5–6.

Naya, Seiji, and others. 1989. *ASEAN-U.S. Initiative: Assessment and Recommendations for Improved Economic Relations.* Honolulu and Singapore: East-West Center and Institute of Southeast Asian Studies.

Nelson, Joan, ed. 1990. *Economic Crisis and Policy Choice.* Princeton University Press.

Nelson, Joan, and Stephanie J. Eglinton. 1992. *Encouraging Democracy: What Role for Conditioned Aid?* Washington: Oversas Development Council.

———. 1993. *Global Goals, Contentious Means: Issues of Multiple Aid Conditionality.* Washington: Overseas Development Council.

Nester, William R. 1992. *Japan and the Third World: Patterns, Power, Prospects.* St. Martin's Press.

Nicolaides, Phedon. 1990. "Responding to European Integration: Developing Countries and Services." *Journal of Common Market Studies* 29 (December): 201–15.

Nivola, Pietro S. 1993. *Regulating Unfair Trade.* Brookings.

Nogues, Julio. 1990. "Patents and Pharmaceutical Drugs: Understanding the Pressures on Developing Countries." *Journal of World Trade* 24 (December): 81–104.

Nogués, Julio, and Neera Gulati. 1992. "Economic Policies and Performance under Alternative Trade Regimes: Latin America during the 1980s." LAC Technical Department Report 16. Washington: World Bank, Latin America and Caribbean Region.

Organization for Economic Cooperation and Development. 1989. *Development Co-Operation: Efforts and Policies of the Members of the Development Assistance Committee, 1989.* Paris.

———. 1991. *Development Co-Operation: Efforts and Policies of the Members of the Development Assistance Committee, 1991.* Paris.

———. 1992. *Integrating the Developing Countries into the International Trading System.* Paris.

Ostry, Sylvia. 1990. *Governments and Corporations in a Shrinking World.* New York: Council on Foreign Relations.

Ostry, Sylvia, and Richard R. Nelson. 1995. *Techno-Nationalism and Techno-Gobalism: Conflict and Cooperation.* Brookings.

Oye, Kenneth. 1992. *Economic Discrimination and Political Exchange: World Political Economy in the 1930s and 1980s.* Princeton University Press.

Oyejide, T. Ademola. 1990. "The Participation of Developing Countries in the Uruguay Round: An African Perspective." *World Economy* 13 (September): 427–44.

Pack, Howard, and Larry E. Westphal. 1986. "Industrial Strategy and Technological Change: Theory vs. Reality." *Journal of Development Economics* 22 (June): 87–128.

Page, Sheila. 1992. "Some Implications of Europe 1992 for Developing Countries." Technical Paper 60. Paris: OECD Development Centre.

Pangestu, Mari, Hadi Soesastro, and Mubariq Ahmad. 1992. "A New Look at Intra-ASEAN Economic Cooperation." *ASEAN Economic Bulletin* 8 (March): 333–52.

Papageorgiu, Demetris, Michael Michaely, and Armeane M. Choksi. 1991. *Liberalizing Foreign Trade,* vol. 1, *The Experience of Argentina, Chile, and Uruguay.* Cambridge: Basil Blackwell.

Park, Yung Chul, and Won Am Park. Forthcoming. "Capital Movements, Real Asset Speculation, and Macroeconomic Adjustment in Korea." In Sebastian

Edwards, ed., *Capital Controls, Exchange Rates and Monetary Policy in the World Economy.* Cambridge University Press.

Pastor, Manuel, and Carol Wise. 1994. "The Origins and Sustainability of Mexico's Free Trade Policy." *International Organization* 48 (Summer): 459–89.

Pastor, Robert. 1990. "Salinas Takes a Gamble." *New Republic,* September 10 and 17, 27–32.

Perot, Ross, and Pat Choate. 1993. *Save Your Job, Save Our Country: Why NAFTA Must be Stopped—Now!* New York: Hyperion.

Petrazzini, Ben A. 1993. "Foreign Direct Investment in Latin America's Privatization." In *Latin America's Turnaround: Privatization, Foreign Investment and Growth,* edited by Paul H. Boeker, 55–96. San Francisco: ICS Press.

Petri, Peter. 1993. "The East Asian Trading Bloc: An Analytical History." In *Regionalism and Rivalry: Japan and the United States in Pacific Asia,* edited by Jeffrey A. Frankel and Miles Kahler, 21–52. University of Chicago Press.

Przeworski, Adam, and Fernando Limongi. 1993. "Political Regimes and Economic Growth." *Journal of Economic Perspectives* 7 (Summer): 51–69.

Quirk, Peter, and others. 1987. *Floating Exchange Rates in Developing Countries: Experience with Auction and Interbank Markets.* Occasional Paper 53. Washington: International Monetary Fund.

Randhawa, P. S. 1987. "Punta del Este and After: Negotiations on Trade in Services and the Uruguay Round." *Journal of World Trade Law* 21 (August): 163–72.

Ravenhill, John. 1985. *Collective Clientelism: The Lomé Conventions and North-South Relations.* Columbia University Press.

Rix, Alan. 1993a. *Japan's Foreign Aid Challenge.* New York: Routledge.

———. 1993b. "Managing Japan's Aid: ASEAN." In *Japan's Foreign Aid: Power and Policy in a New Era,* edited by Bruce Koppel and Robert M. Orr, Jr., 19–40. Boulder: Westview Press.

Rodrik, Dani. 1989. "Promises, Promises: Credible Policy Reform via Signalling." *Economic Journal* 99 (September): 756–72.

———. 1994. "The Rush to Free Trade in the Developing World: Why So Late? Why Now? Will It Last?" In *Voting for Reform: Political Liberalization, Democracy and Economic Adjustment,* edited by Stephan Haggard and Steven B. Webb, 61–88. New York: Oxford University Press.

Roy, Ramashray. 1993. "India in 1992: Search for Safety." *Asian Survey* 33 (February): 119–28.

Sachs, Jeffrey. 1987. "Trade and Exchange Rate Policies in Trade-Oriented Adjustment Programs." In Vittorio Corbo, Morris Goldstein, and Mohsin Khan, eds., *Growth-Oriented Adjustment Programs.* Washington: International Monetary Fund.

———, ed. 1989. *Developing Country Debt and the World Economy.* University of Chicago Press.

Salacluse, Jeswald W. 1990. "BIT by BIT: The Growth of Bilateral Investment Treaties and Their Impact on Foreign Investment in Developing Countries." *International Lawyer* 24 (Fall): 655–76.

Schoppa, Leonard. 1993. "Two-Level Games and Bargaining Outcomes: Why *Gaiatsu* Succeeds in Japan in Some Cases but Not Others." *International Organization* 47 (Summer): 353–86.

Schott, Jeffrey, ed. 1989. *Free Trade Areas and U.S. Trade Policy.* Washington: Institute for International Economics.

———. 1991. "Trading Blocs and the World System." *World Economy* 14 (March): 1–17

Stallings, Barbara. 1992. "International Influence on Economic Policy: Debt, Stabilization and Structural Reform." In *The Politics of Adjustment,* edited by Stephan Haggard and Robert Kaufman, 41–88. Princeton University Press.

Sutton, Michael. 1992. "Euro-Maghreb Partnership: A New Form of Association?" In Economist Intelligence Unit, *European Trends,* 61–67, n. 3. London.

Svensson, Lars. 1993. "Fixed Exchange Rates as a Means to Price Stability: What Have We Learned?" NBER Working Paper 4504. (October).

Takahashi, Akira. 1993. "From Reparations to Katagawari: Japan's ODA to the Philippines." In *Japan's Foreign Aid: Power and Policy in a New Era,* edited by Bruce Koppel and Robert M. Orr, Jr., 63–90. Boulder: Westview Press.

Thomas, T. 1994. "Change in Climate to Foreign Investment in India." *Columbia Journal of World Business* (Spring): 32–40.

Thomas, Christopher, and Greg A. Tereposky. 1993. "The Evolving Relationship between Trade and Environmental Regulation." *Journal of World Trade* 27 (August): 23–45.

Trachtman, Joel P. 1992. "GATT Dispute Settlement Panel: United States— Restrictions on Imports of Tuna." *American Journal of International Law* 86 (January): 142–51.

Tyson, Laura. 1992. *Who's Bashing Whom? Trade Conflict in High-Technology Industries.* Washington: Institute for International Economics.

Unger, Danny. 1993. "Japan's Capital Exports: Molding East Asia." In *Japan's Emerging Global Role,* edited by Danny Unger and Paul Blackburn, 155–70. Boulder: Lynne Rienner.

United Nations Conference on Trade And Development. 1992a. *UNCTAD Commodity Yearbook, 1992.* Geneva.

———. 1992b. *Handbook of Trade and Development Statistics.* Geneva.

———. 1993. *UNCTAD Trade and Development Report, 1993.* Geneva.

U.S. Congress. 1988. Hearings before the Subcommittee on International Economic Policy and Trade of the House Committee on Foreign Affairs. 100 Cong. 2 sess. February 25 and March 16. Washington.

U.S. Department of Commerce. 1985. *Study of Foreign Government Targeting Practices and the Remedies Available under the Countervailing Duty and Antidumping Duty Laws.* Washington.

U.S. Department of the Treasury. 1990. *National Treatment Study: Report to Congress on Foreign Government Treatment of U.S. Commercial Banking and Securities Organizations.* Washington.

U.S. International Trade Commission. 1987. *Operations of the Trade Agreements Program. 38th Report 1986.* Washington: Government Printing Office.

———. 1988. *Operation of the Trade Agreements Program: 39th Report 1987*. Washington: GPO.

———. 1989. *Operation of the Trade Agreements Program: 40th Report 1988*. Washington: GPO.

———. 1990. *Operation of the Trade Agreements Program: 41st Report 1989*. Washington: GPO.

———. 1991. *Operation of the Trade Agreements Program: 42nd Report 1990*. Washington: GPO.

———. 1992. *The Year in Trade: Operation of the Trade Agreements Program 1991: 43rd Report 1991*. Washington: GPO.

———. 1993. *The Year in Trade 1992: Operation of the Trade Agreements Program: 44th Report*. Washington: GPO.

U.S. Trade Representative. 1985a. *Report on Foreign Industrial Targeting*. Washington.

———. 1985b. *Selected Problems Encountered by U.S. Services Industries in Trade in Services*. September 6. Washington.

———. 1993. "Section 301 Table of Cases." September 1. Washington.

———. Various years. *National Trade Estimate Report on Foreign Trade Barriers*. Washington.

Uphoff, Elisabeth. 1990. *Intellectual Property and U.S. Relations with Indonesia, Malaysia, Singapore and Thailand*. Ithaca: Cornell Southeast Asia Program.

Wade, Robert. 1990. *Governing the Market*. Princeton University Press.

Webb, Steven B., and Karim Shariff. 1992. "Designing and Implementing Adjustment Programs." In *Adjustment Lending Revisited: Policies to Restore Growth*, edited by Vittorio Corbo, Stanley Fischer, and Steven B. Webb, 69–92. Washington: World Bank.

Westphal, Larry E. 1990. "Industrial Policy in an Export-Propelled Economy: Lessons from South Korea's Experience." *Journal of Economic Perspectives* 4 (Summer): 41–59.

Winglee, Peter, and others. 1992. *Issues and Developments in International Trade Policy*. Washington: International Monetary Fund.

Williamson, John, ed. 1990. *Latin American Adjustment: How Much Has Happened?* Washington: Institute for International Economics.

———. ed. 1993. *The Political Economy of Economic Policy Reform* Washington: Institute for International Economics.

Winham, Gilbert R. 1986. *International Trade and the Tokyo Round Negotiations*. Princeton University Press.

———. 1988. "Why Canada Acted." In *Bilateralism, Multilateralism and Canada in U.S. Trade Policy*, edited by William Diebold, Jr., 37–54. Ballinger Publishing Co.

———. 1989. "The Prenegotiation Phase of the Uruguay Round." *International Journal* 44 (Spring): 280–303.

Wise, Carol. 1994. "The Politics of Peruvian Economic Reform: Overcoming Legacies of State-Led Development." *Journal of Interamerican Studies and World Affairs* 36: 75–125.

Wolf, Martin. 1987a. "Two-Edged Sword: Demands of Developing Countries and the Trading System." In *Power, Passions and Purpose: Prospects for North-*

South Negotiations, edited by Jagdish Bhagwati and John Gerard Ruggie, 201–29. Columbia University Press.

———. 1987b. "Differential and More Favorable Treatment of Developing Countries in the International Trading System," *World Bank Economic Review* 1 (September): 647–68.

Wonnacott, Ronald J. 1991. *The Economics of Overlapping Free Trade Areas and the Mexican Challenge.* Toronto and Washington: C.D. Howe and the National Planning Association.

World Bank. 1987. *World Debt Tables 1986–87.* Washington.

———. 1990. *World Debt Tables 1989–90.* Washington.

———. 1993a. *Latin America and the Caribbean: A Decade after the Debt Crisis.* Washington, Latin America and Caribbean Region.

———. 1993b. *The East Asian Miracle: Economic Growth and Public Policy.* Oxford University Press.

———. 1993c. *World Debt Tables 1992–93.* Washington.

Yamazawa, Ippei. 1992. "On Pacific Economic Integration." *The Economic Journal* 102 (November): 1519–29.

Yoffie, David. 1983. *Power and Protectionism.* Columbia University Press.

Zartman, I. William. 1971. *The Politics of Trade Negotiations between Africa and the European Community: The Weak Confront the Strong.* Princeton University Press.

Zimmerman, Robert F. 1993. *Dollars, Diplomacy and Dependency.* Boulder: Lynne Rienner.

Index

167